Collins

11+
Spatial Reasoning

Quick Practice Tests
Ages 10-11

Faisal Nasim

Contents

ACKNOWLEDGEMENTS

The author and publisher are grateful to the copyright holders for permission to use quoted materials and images.

Every effort has been made to trace copyright holders and obtain their permission for the use of copyright material. The author and publisher will gladly receive information enabling them to rectify any error or omission in subsequent editions. All facts are correct at time of going to press.

Published by Collins
An imprint of HarperCollins*Publishers* Limited
1 London Bridge Street
London SE1 9GF

HarperCollins*Publishers*
Macken House, 39/40 Mayor Street Upper,
Dublin 1, D01 C9W8, Ireland

ISBN: 9781844199204

First published 2018
This edition published 2020
Previously published by Letts

10 9

British Library Cataloguing in Publication Data.

A CIP record of this book is available from the British Library.

Author and Series Editor: Faisal Nasim
Commissioning Editor: Michelle I'Anson
Editor and Project Manager: Sonia Dawkins
Cover Design: Sarah Duxbury and Kevin Robbins
Text and Page Design: Ian Wrigley
Layout and Artwork: Q2A Media
Production: Natalia Rebow
Printed in the UK, by Ashford Colour Press Ltd.

Please note that Collins is not associated with CEM in any way. This book does not contain any official questions and it is not endorsed by CEM.

Our question types are based on those set by CEM, but we cannot guarantee that your child's actual 11+ exam will contain the same question types or format as this book.

MIX
Paper | Supporting responsible forestry
FSC™ C007454

This book contains FSC™ certified paper and other controlled sources to ensure responsible forest management.

For more information visit: www.harpercollins.co.uk/green

About this book

Familiarisation with 11+ test-style questions is a critical step in preparing your child for the 11+ selection tests. This book gives children lots of opportunities to test themselves in short, manageable bursts, helping to build confidence and improve the chance of test success.

It contains 25 tests designed to build key spatial reasoning skills.

- Each test is designed to be completed within a short amount of time. Frequent, short bursts of revision are found to be more productive than lengthier sessions.

- CEM tests often consist of a series of shorter, time-pressured sections so these practice tests will help your child become accustomed to this style of questioning.

- If your child does not complete any of the tests in the allocated time, they may need further practice in that area.

- We recommend your child uses a pencil to complete the tests, so that they can rub out the answers and try again at a later date if necessary.

- Children will need a pencil and a rubber to complete the tests and some spare paper for rough working. They will also need to be able to see a clock/watch and should have a quiet place in which to do the tests.

- Answers to every question are provided at the back of the book, with explanations given where appropriate.

- After completing the tests, children should revisit their weaker areas and attempt to improve their scores and timings.

Download a free progress chart from our website

collins.co.uk/11plus

Test 1

You have 6 minutes to complete this test.

You have 12 questions to complete within the given time.

In each question, circle the letter below the set of blocks that can be combined to make the figure on the left.

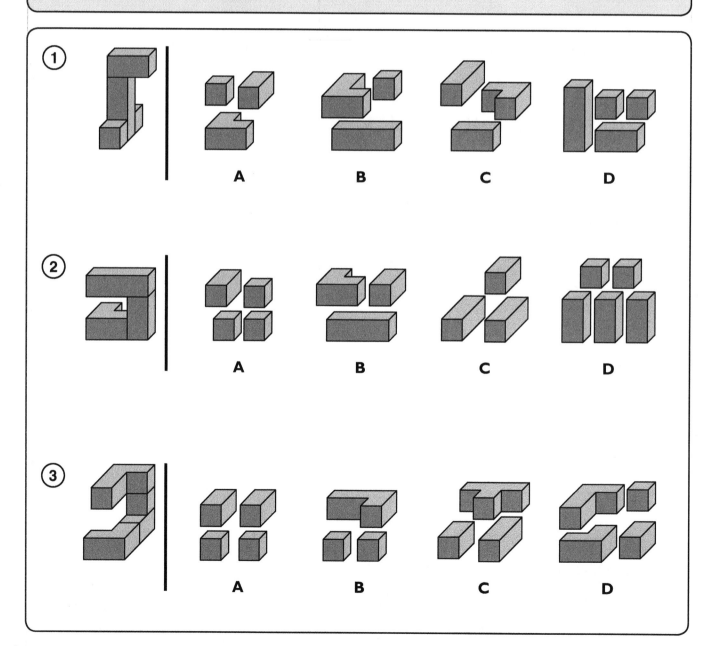

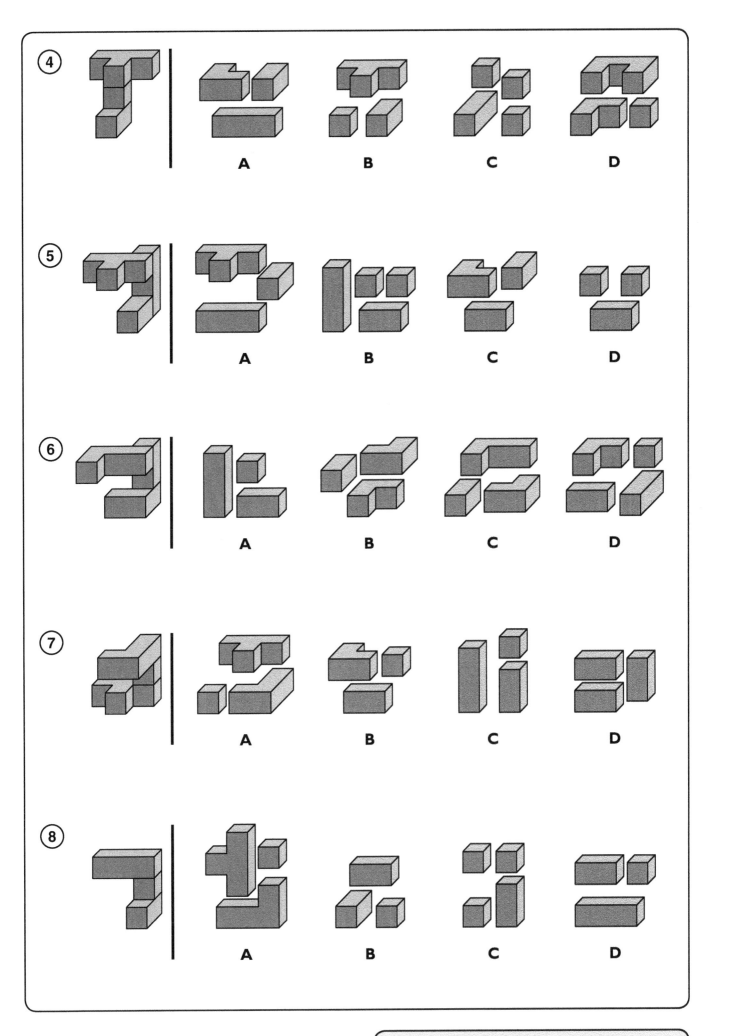

Questions continue on next page

5

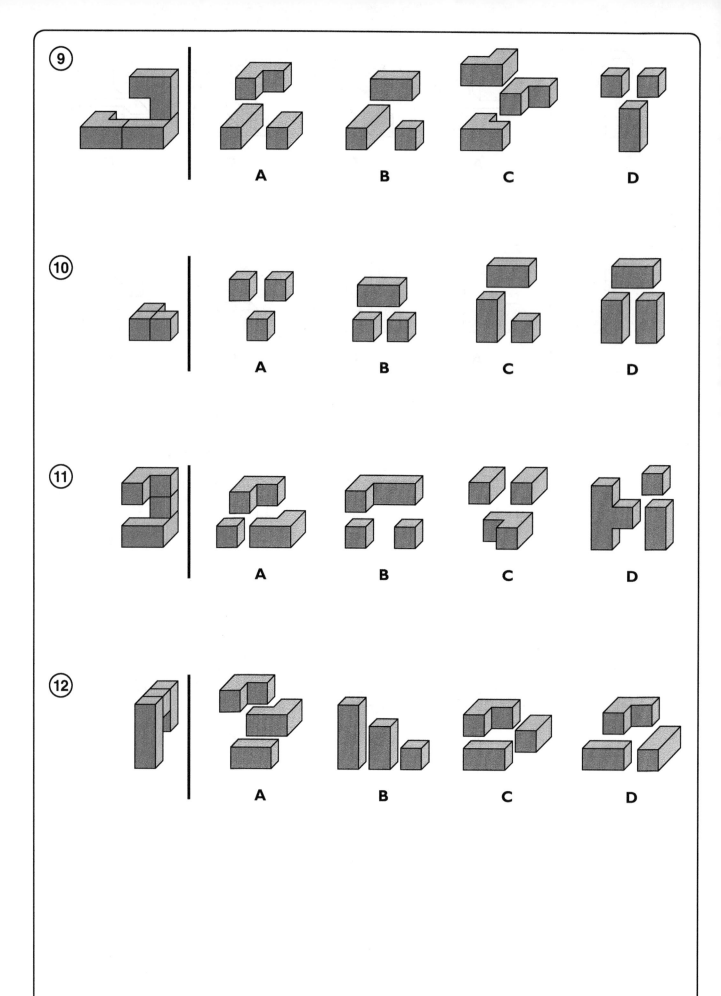

Test 2

You have 5 minutes to complete this test.

You have 10 questions to complete within the given time.

In each question, circle the letter below the figure that can be combined with the first figure to create the shape in the grey box. The first figure must not be rotated.

EXAMPLE

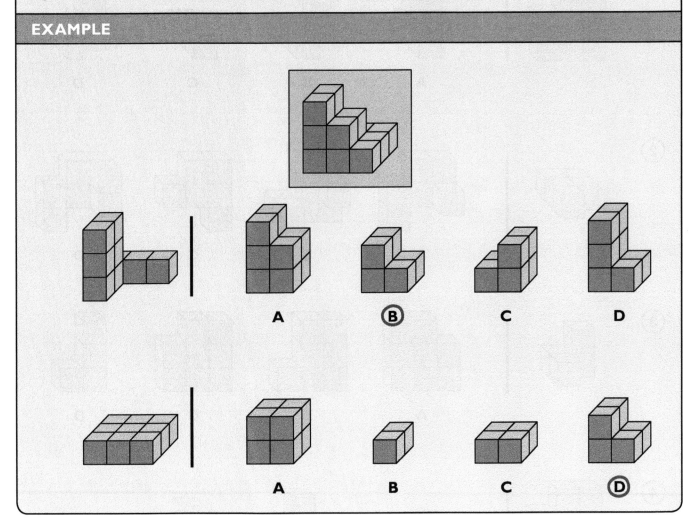

Questions start on next page

Refer to the shape in the grey box for Questions 1–5 below.

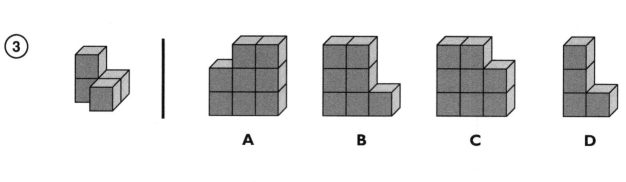

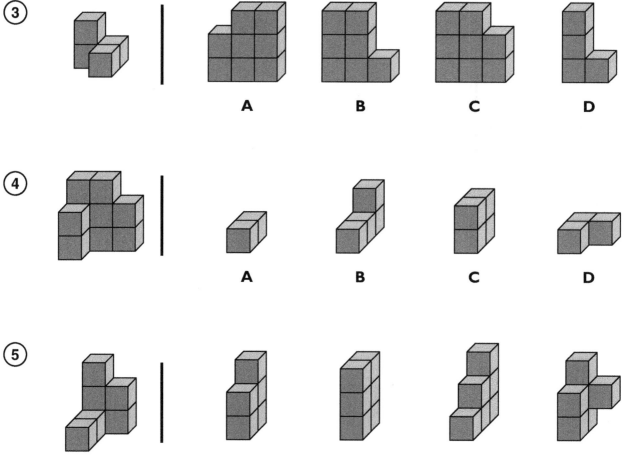

Refer to the shape in the grey box for Questions 6–10 below.

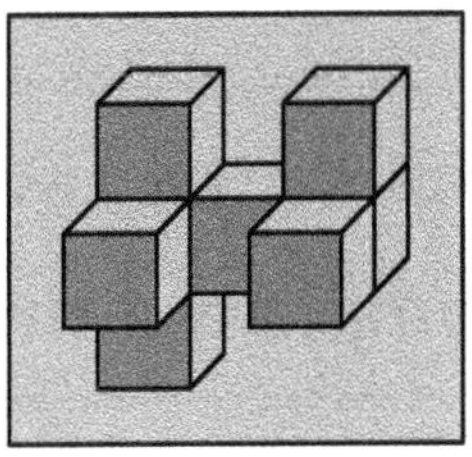

(6)

A   B   C   D

(7)

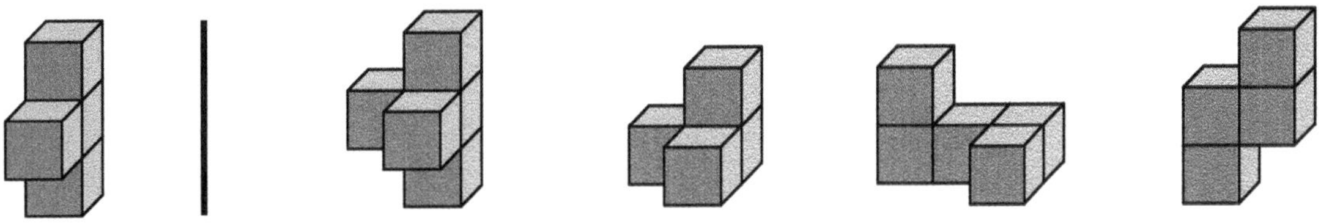

A   B   C   D

(8)

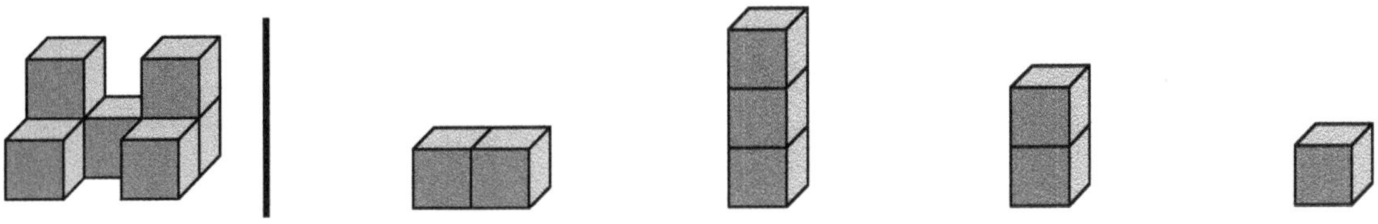

A   B   C   D

(9)

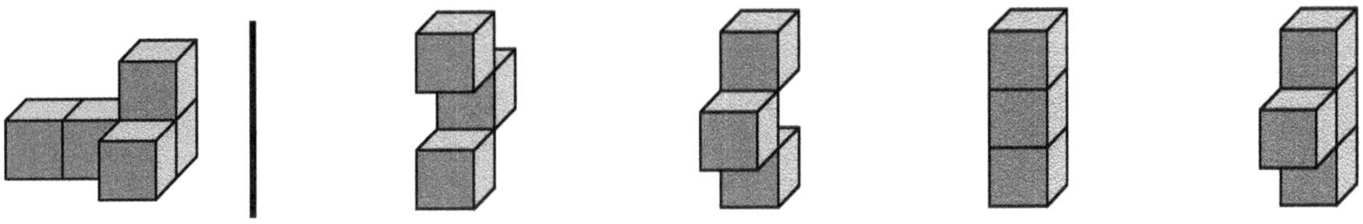

A   B   C   D

(10)

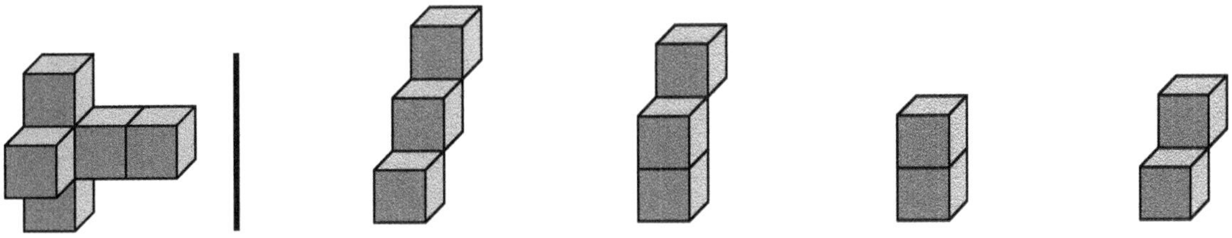

A   B   C   D

Score: .... / 10

9

Test 3

You have 6 minutes to complete this test.

You have 12 questions to complete within the given time.

In each question, one of the 3D figures below has been rotated to create the figure shown. Circle the letter of the figure that has been rotated.

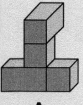

A

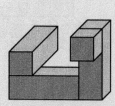

D

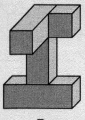

B

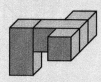

E

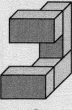

C

F

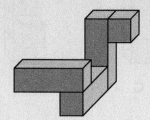

A   Ⓓ

B   E

C   F

①

A	D
B	E
C	F

②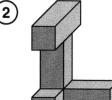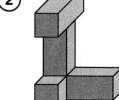

A	D
B	E
C	F

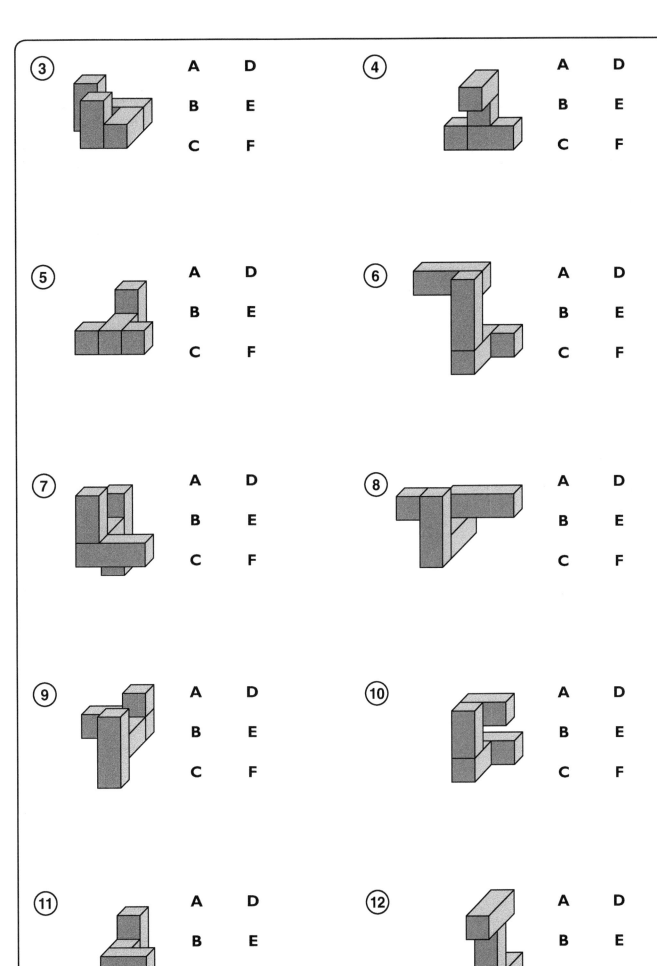

③   A   D
     B   E
     C   F

④   A   D
     B   E
     C   F

⑤   A   D
     B   E
     C   F

⑥   A   D
     B   E
     C   F

⑦   A   D
     B   E
     C   F

⑧   A   D
     B   E
     C   F

⑨   A   D
     B   E
     C   F

⑩   A   D
     B   E
     C   F

⑪   A   D
     B   E
     C   F

⑫   A   D
     B   E
     C   F

Score: .... / 12

Test 4

You have 5 minutes to complete this test.

You have 10 questions to complete within the given time.

In each question, circle the letter below the figure that shows how the left-hand figure will look when folded along the dotted line.

The fold should be made towards the dotted line, not away from it.

EXAMPLE

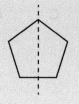

(A) B C D

①

A B C D

②

A B C D

③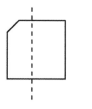

A B C D

④

A B C D

12

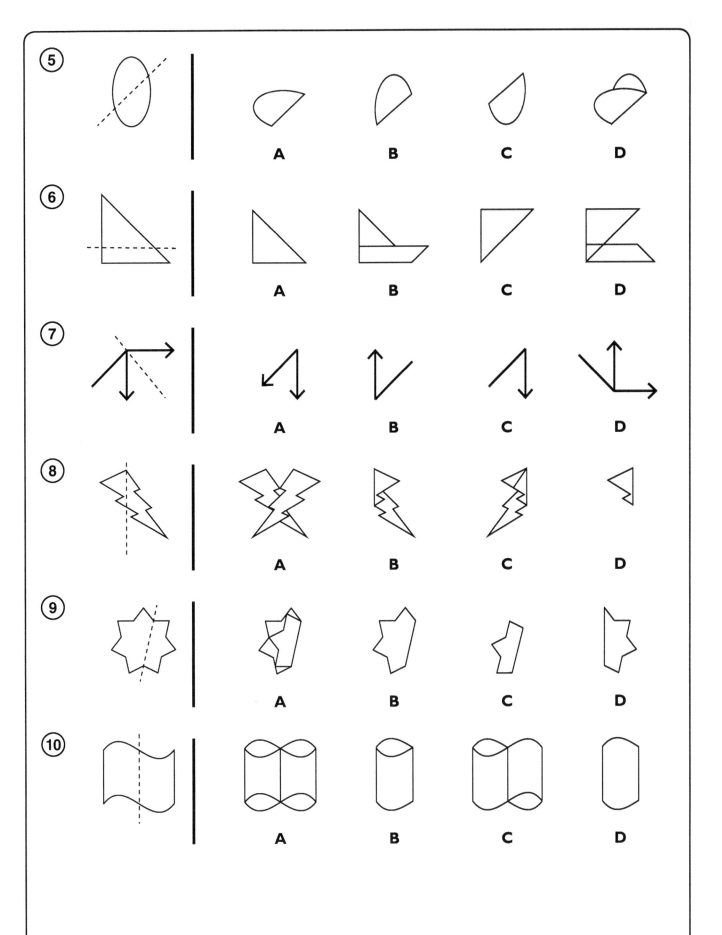

⑤   **A**   **B**   **C**   **D**

⑥   **A**   **B**   **C**   **D**

⑦   **A**   **B**   **C**   **D**

⑧   **A**   **B**   **C**   **D**

⑨   **A**   **B**   **C**   **D**

⑩   **A**   **B**   **C**   **D**

Score: .... / 10

13

Test 5

You have 5 minutes to complete this test.

You have 10 questions to complete within the given time.

In each question, the first row of figures shows how a square is folded and then holes are punched into it.

Circle the letter below the figure that correctly shows the unfolded square.

EXAMPLE

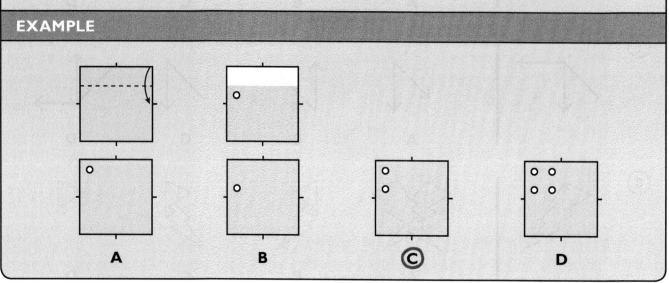

A   B   Ⓒ   D

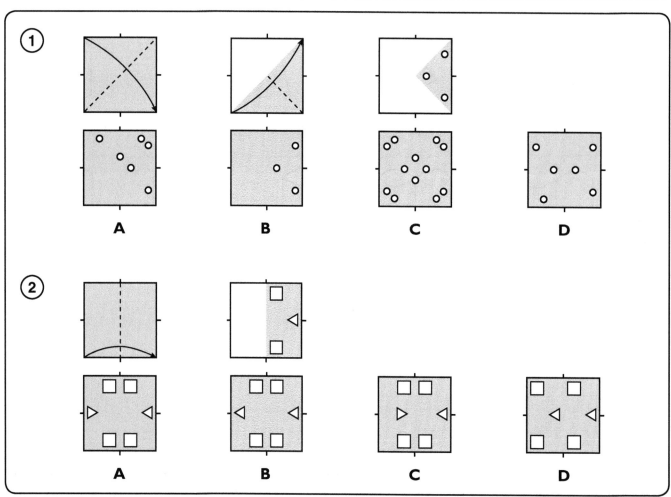

14

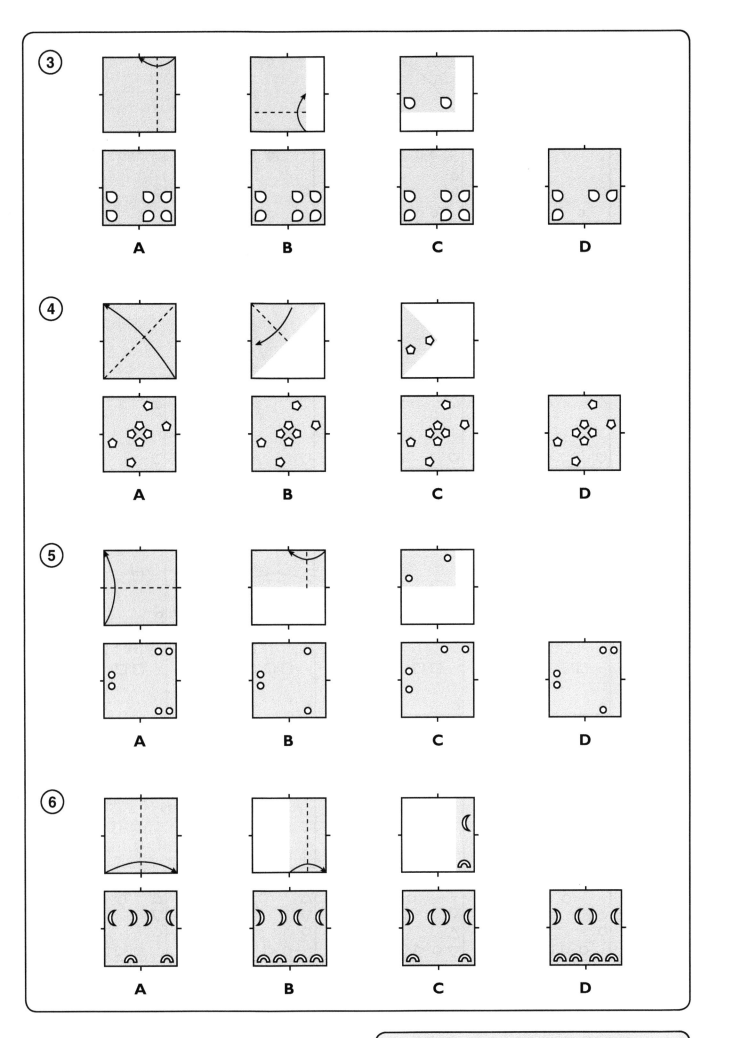

Questions continue on next page

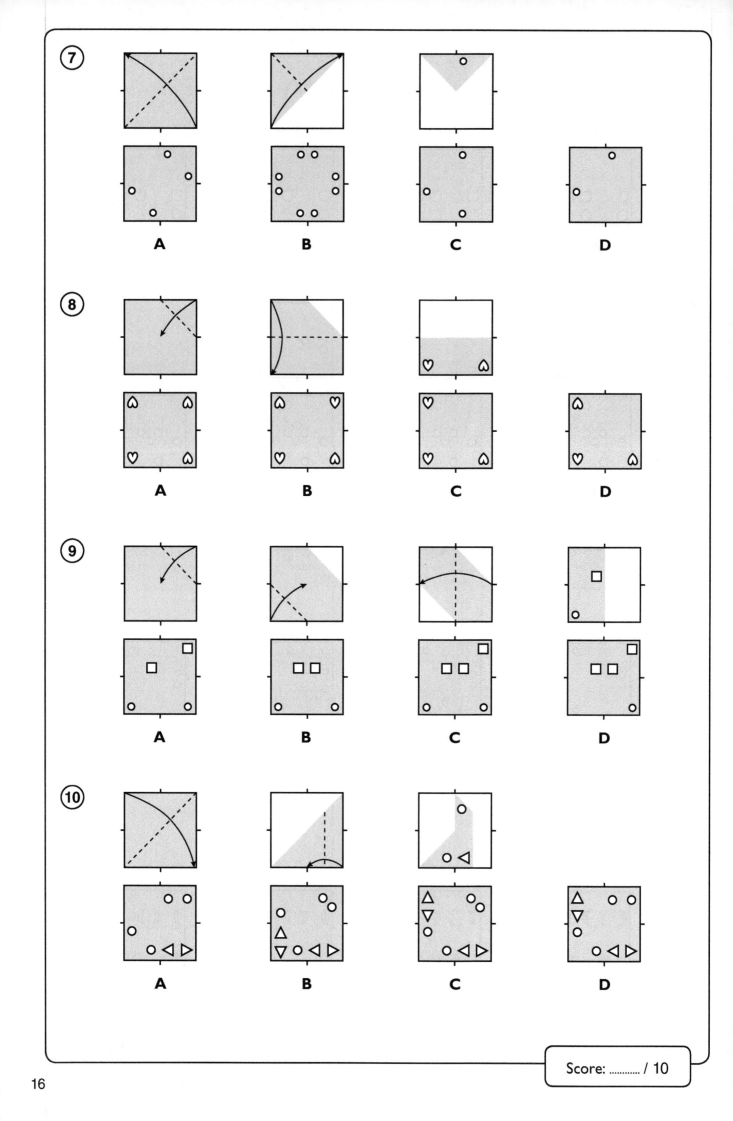

Score: .... / 10

Test 6

You have 5 minutes to complete this test.

You have 10 questions to complete within the given time.

In each question, circle the letter below the figure on the right that shows the <u>top-down 2D view</u> of the 3D figure on the left.

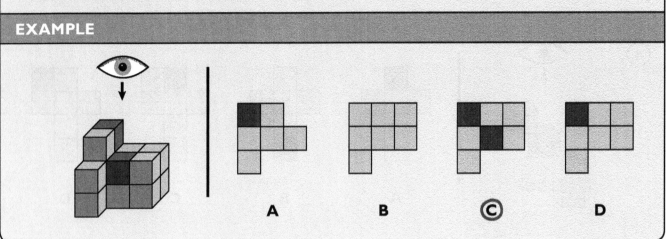

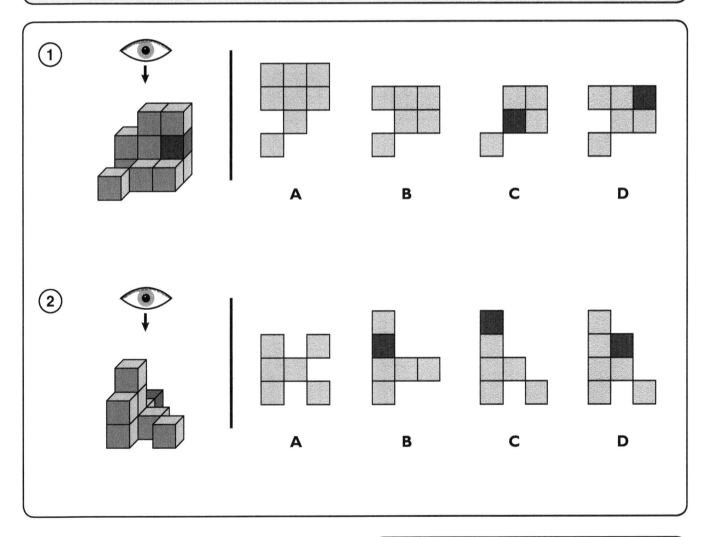

Questions continue on next page

17

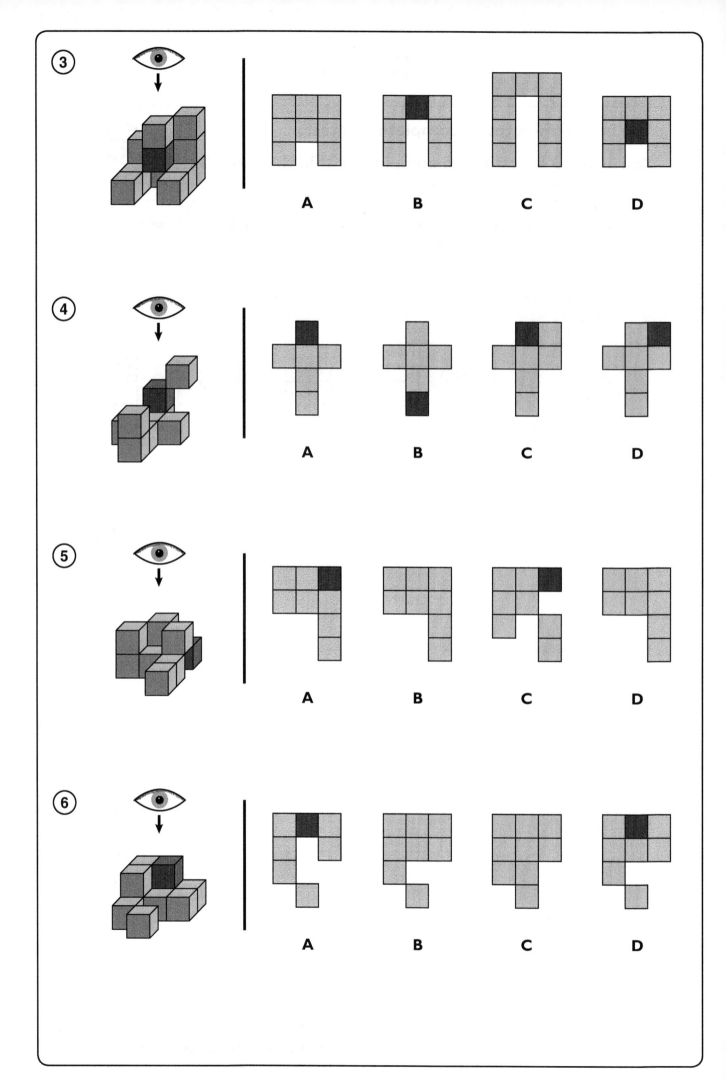

③

A　　　B　　　C　　　D

④

A　　　B　　　C　　　D

⑤

A　　　B　　　C　　　D

⑥

A　　　B　　　C　　　D

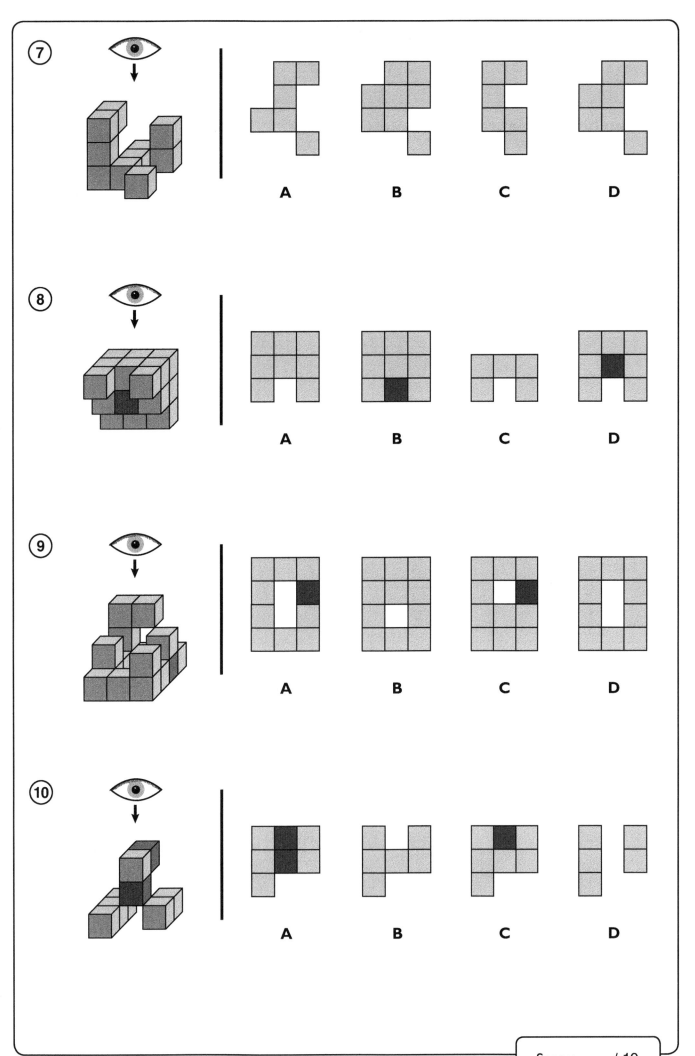

Test 7

You have 5 minutes to complete this test.

You have 10 questions to complete within the given time.

In each question, circle the letter below the figure that shows how the 3D figure on the left could look when viewed looking <u>down from above</u>.

EXAMPLE

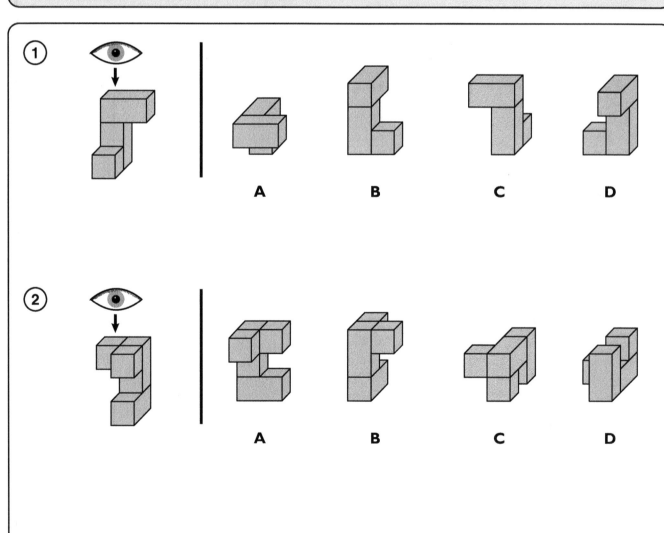

A   Ⓑ   C   D

1

A   B   C   D

2

A   B   C   D

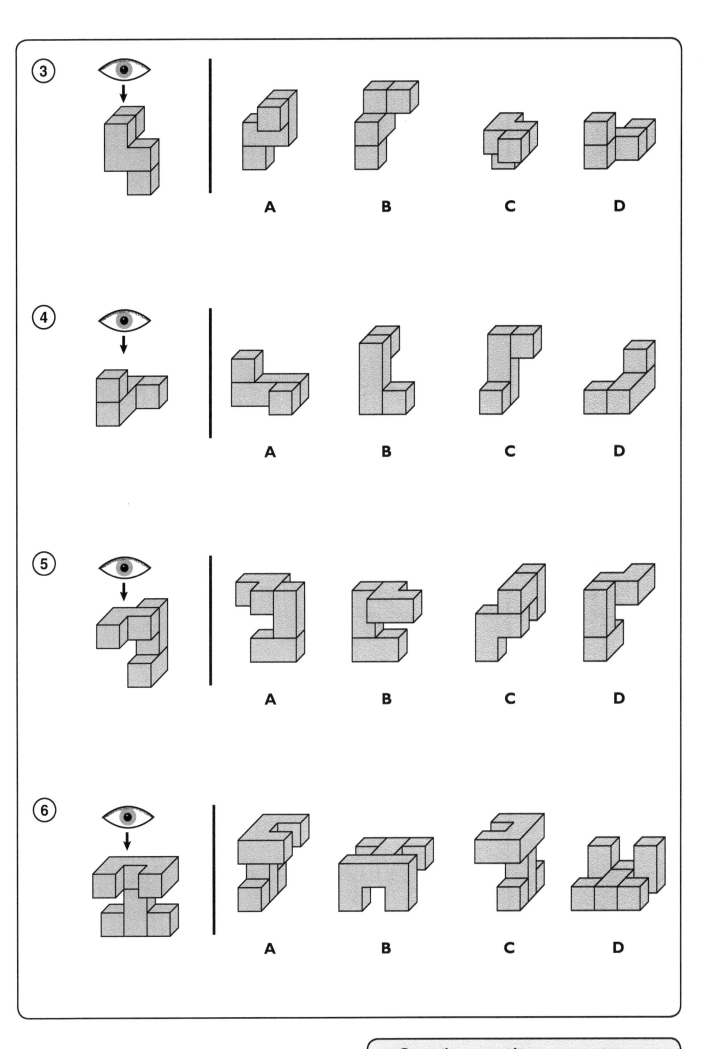

Questions continue on next page

21

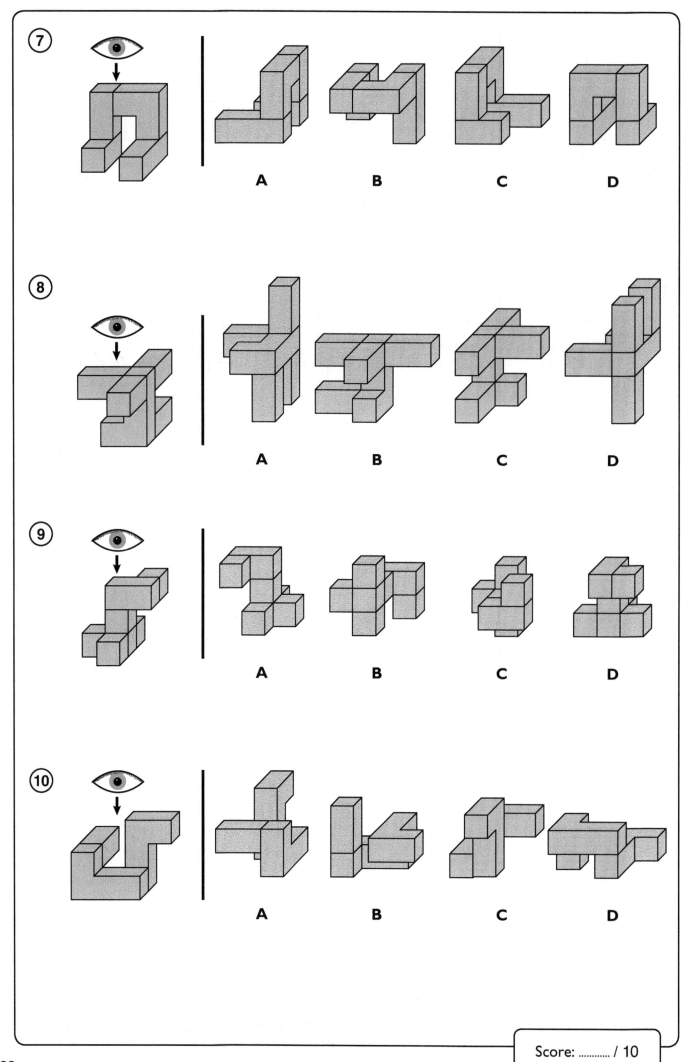

Score: .... / 10

Test 8

You have 5 minutes to complete this test.

You have 10 questions to complete within the given time.

In each question, circle the letter below the cube that can be formed when folding the net on the left.

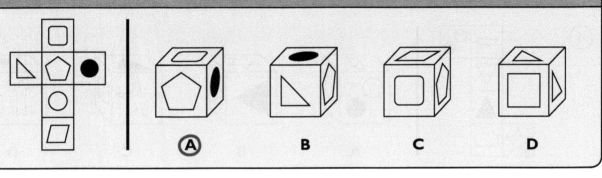

A   B   C   D

A   B   C   D

②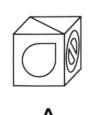

A   B   C   D

Questions continue on next page

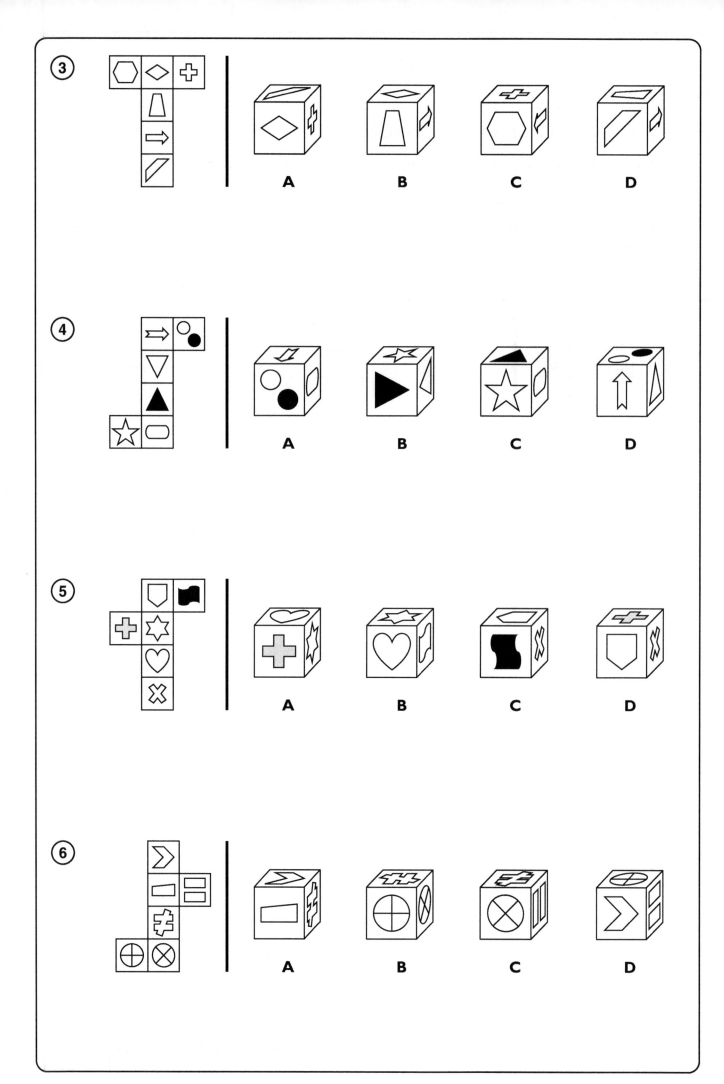

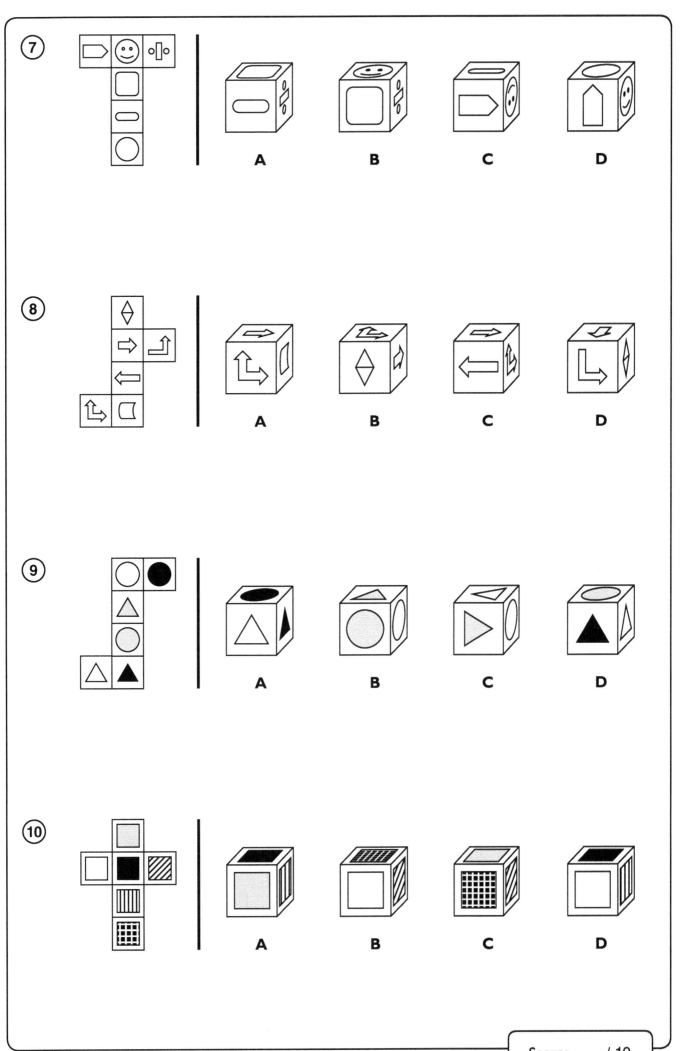

Test 9

You have 4 minutes to complete this test.

You have 8 questions to complete within the given time.

In each question, circle the letter below the net that can be folded to make the cube on the left.

EXAMPLE

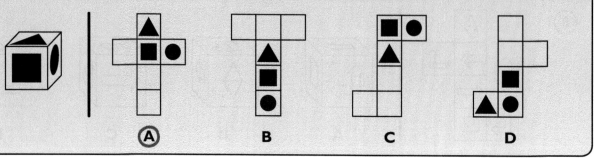

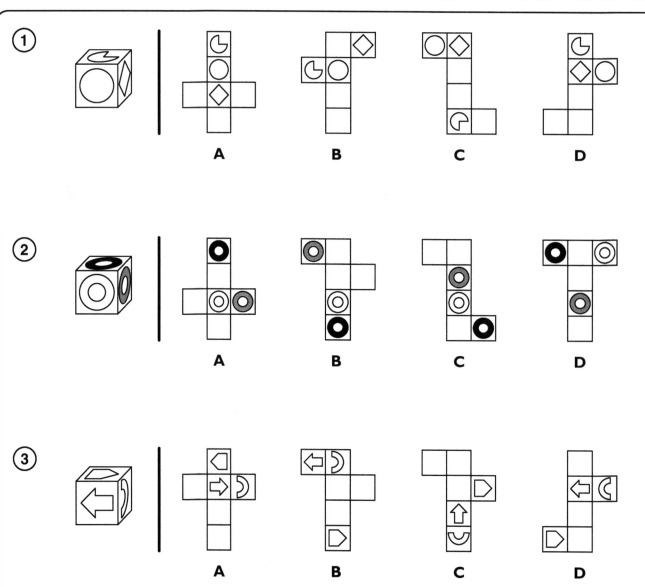

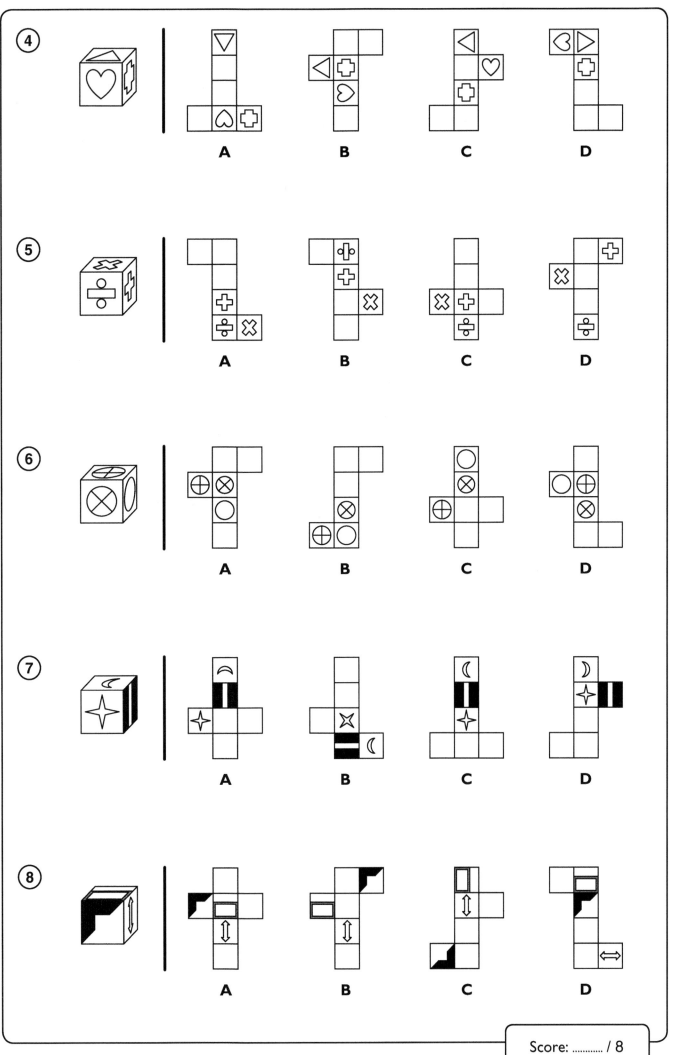

4

A   B   C   D

5

A   B   C   D

6

A   B   C   D

7

A   B   C   D

8

A   B   C   D

Score: .... / 8

Test 10

In each question, circle the letter below the 3D shape that can be formed from the net on the left.

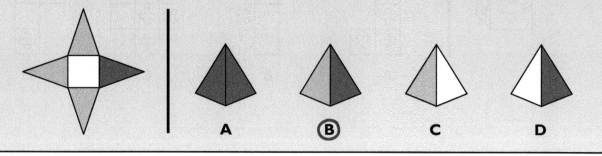

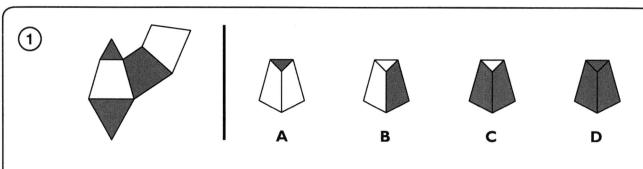

①

②

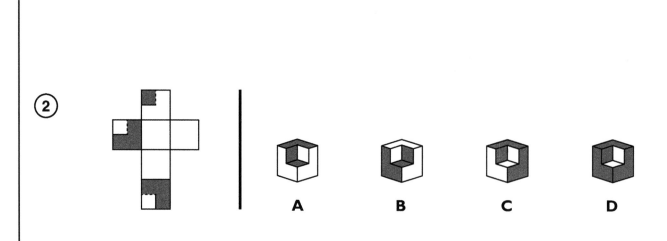

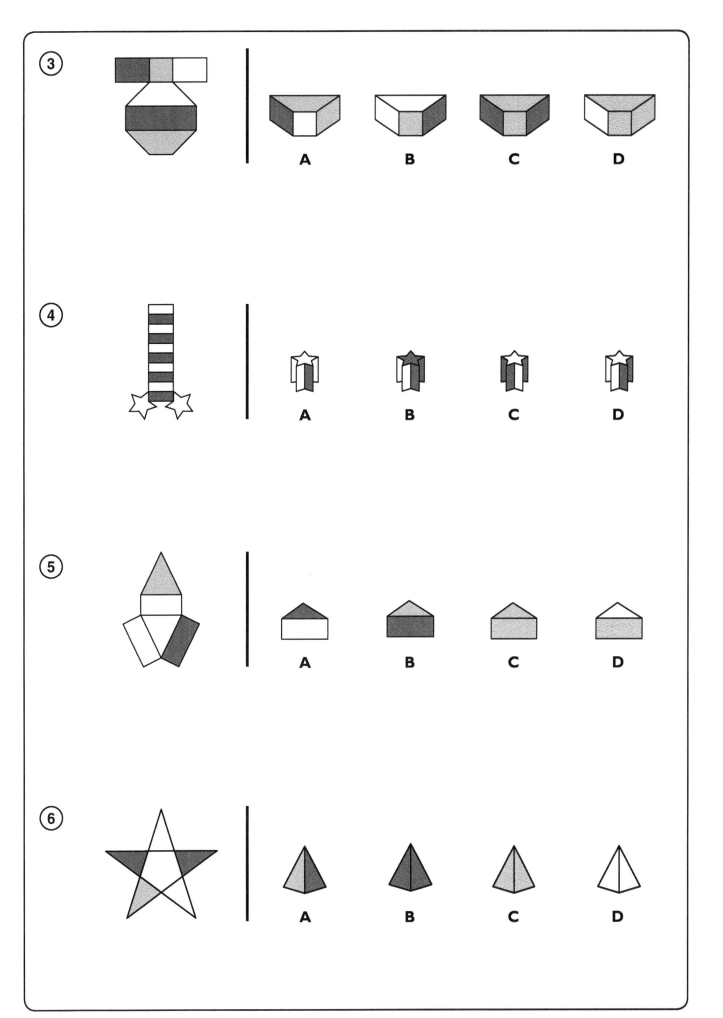

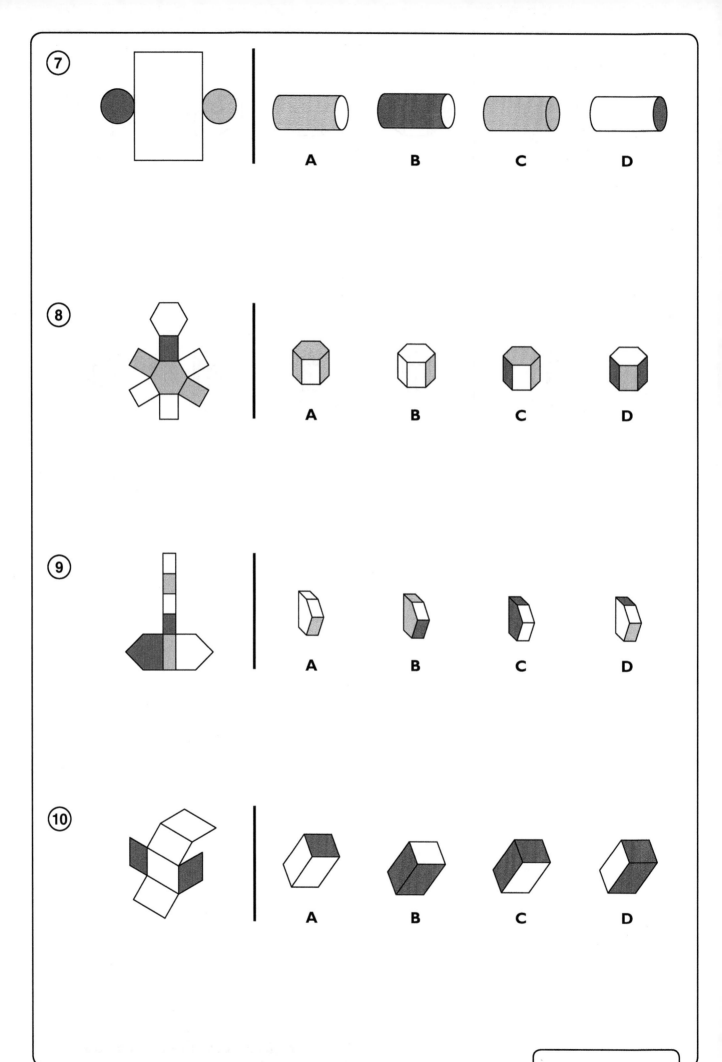

Score: .... / 10

Test 11

You have 5 minutes to complete this test.

You have 10 questions to complete within the given time.

In each question, the figures on the left show different views of the same cube.

Every face of this cube is different.

Circle the letter below the figure that should replace the blank face.

EXAMPLE

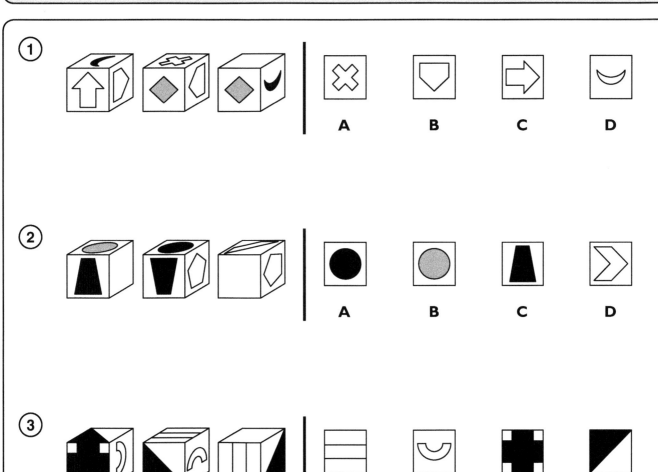

Questions continue on next page

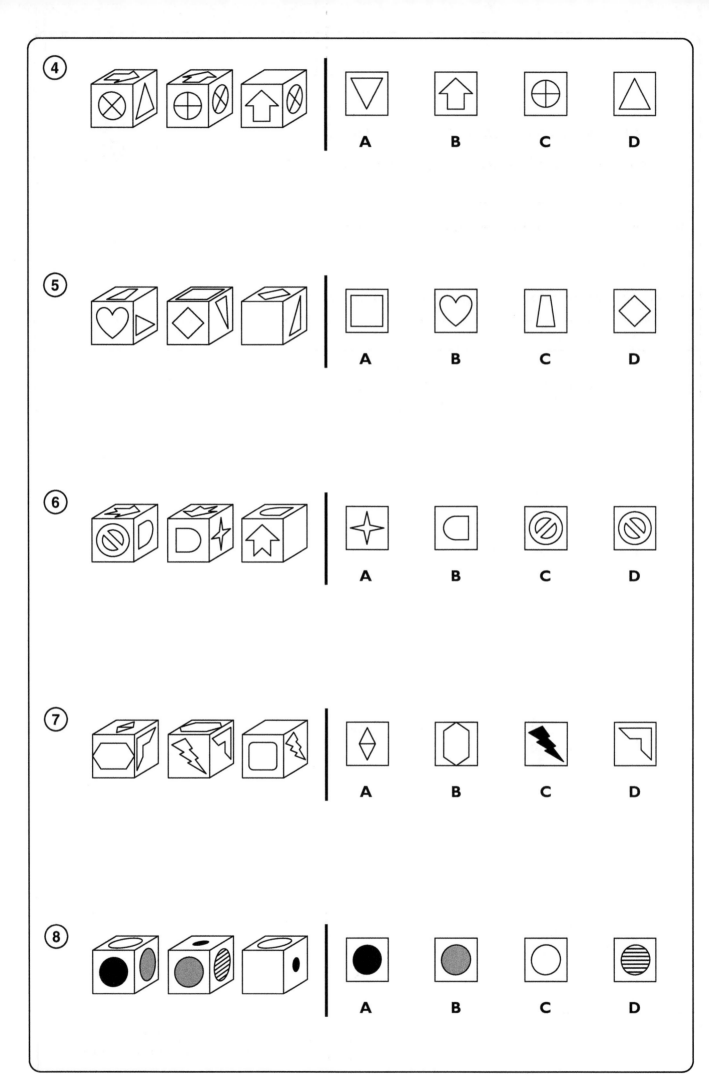

⑨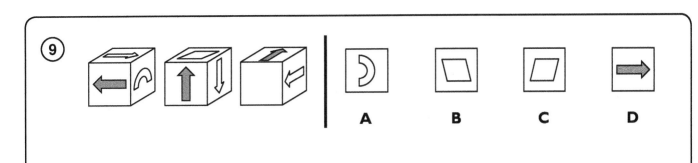

A B C D

⑩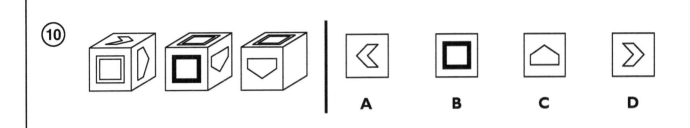

A B C D

Test 12

You have 5 minutes to complete this test.

You have 10 questions to complete within the given time.

In each question, the shape on the left is hidden in one of the figures on the right.

This shape stays exactly the same size and does not get rotated or flipped over.

Circle the letter below the figure that contains the hidden shape.

EXAMPLE

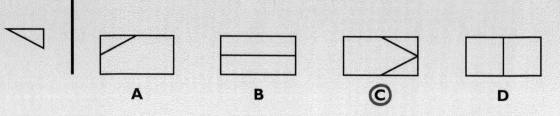

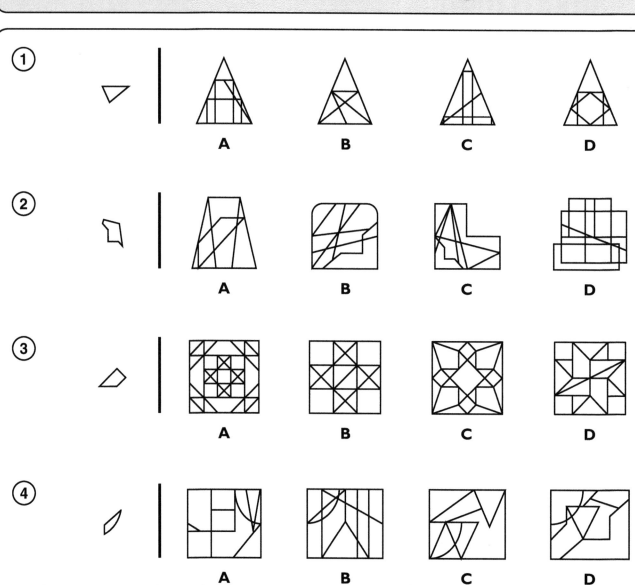

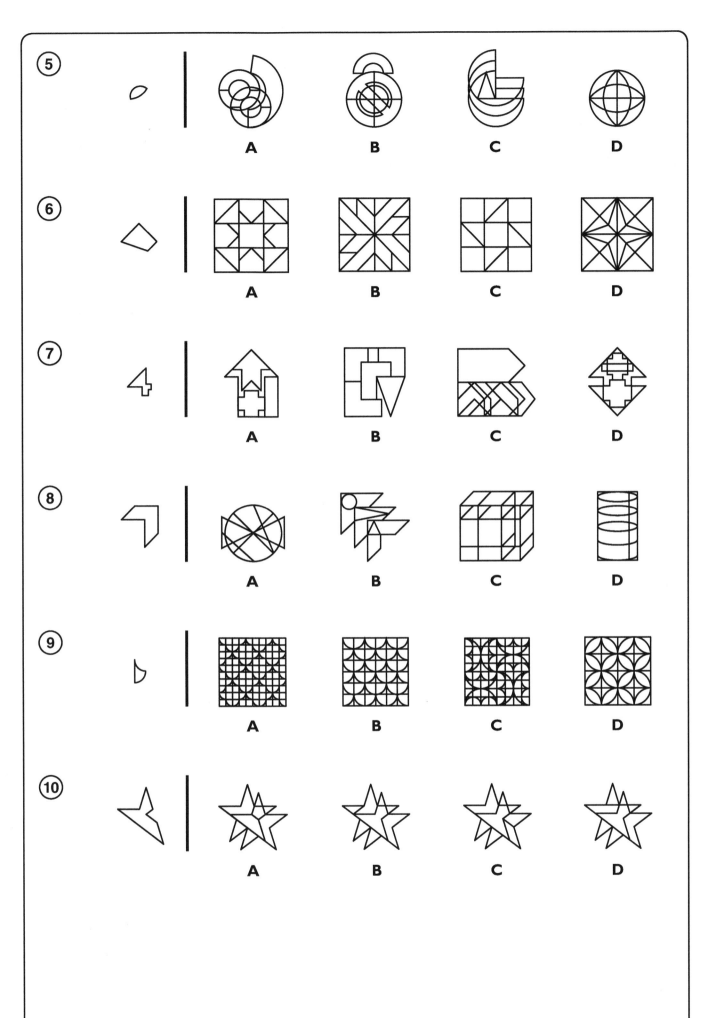

⑤

A   B   C   D

⑥

A   B   C   D

⑦

A   B   C   D

⑧

A   B   C   D

⑨

A   B   C   D

⑩

A   B   C   D

Score: .... / 10

Test 13

You have 6 minutes to complete this test.

You have 12 questions to complete within the given time.

In each question, circle the letter below the set of blocks that can be combined to make the figure on the left.

EXAMPLE

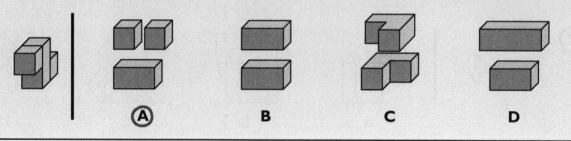

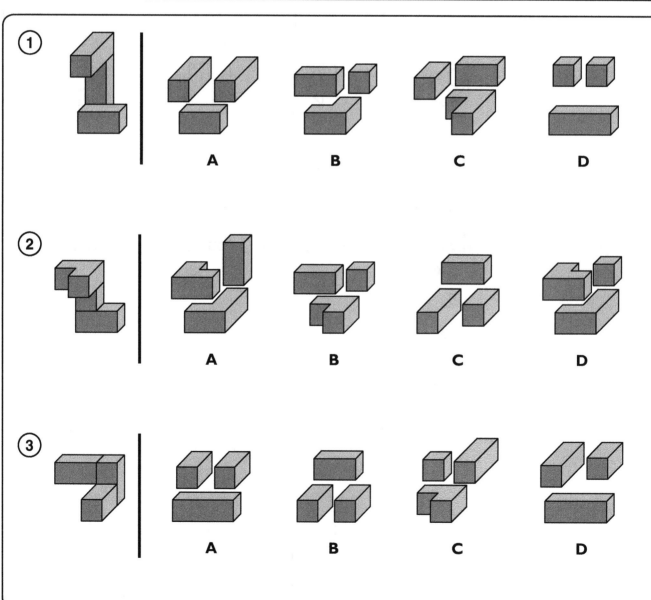

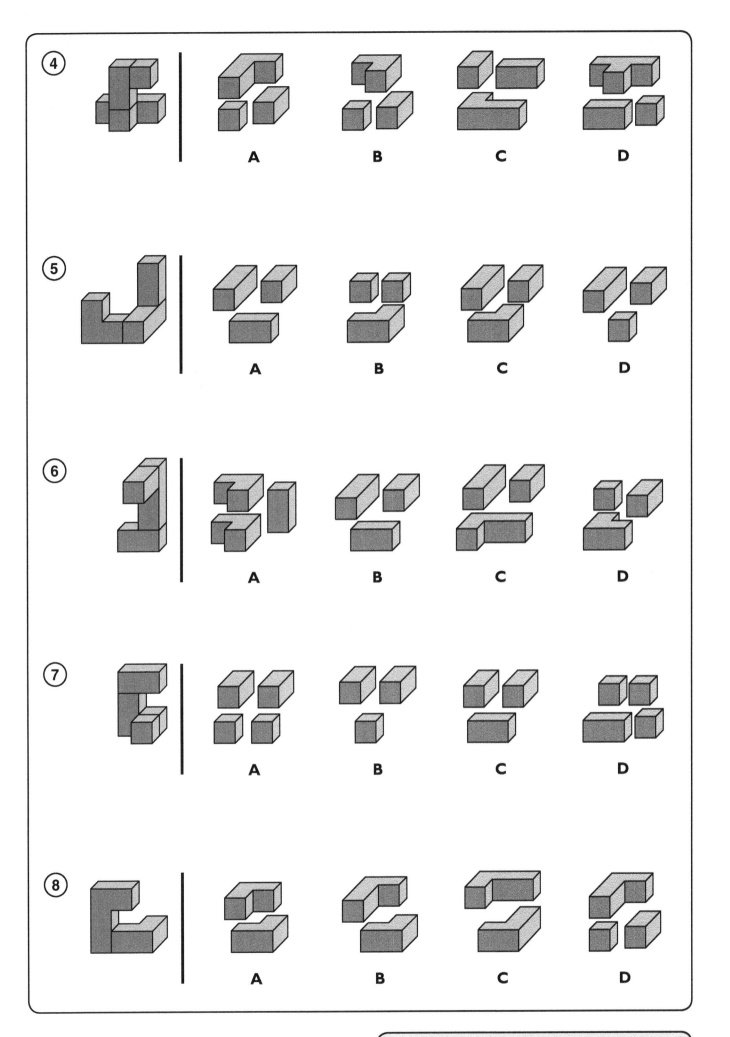

Questions continue on next page

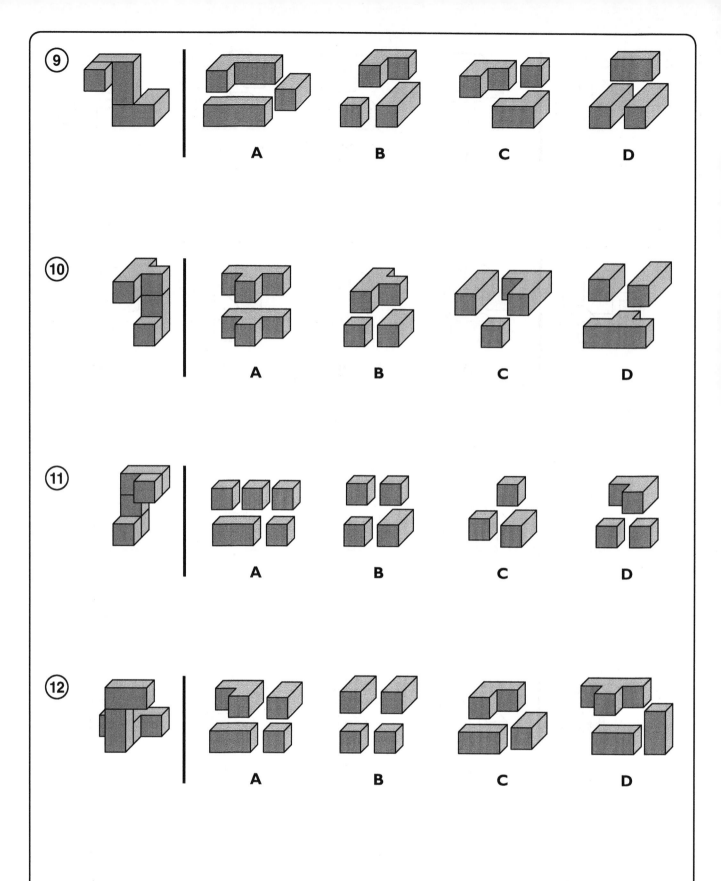

Test 14

You have 5 minutes to complete this test.

You have 10 questions to complete within the given time.

In each question, circle the letter below the figure that can be combined with the first figure to create the shape in the grey box. The first figure must not be rotated.

EXAMPLE

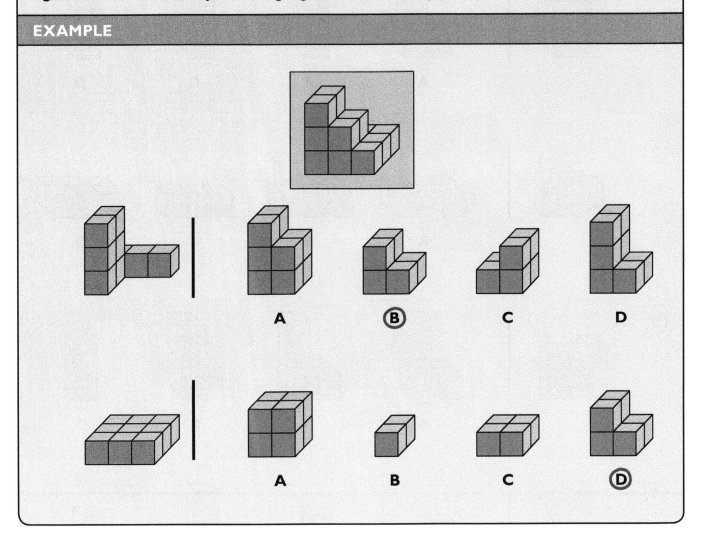

Questions start on next page

Refer to the shape in the grey box for Questions 1–5 below.

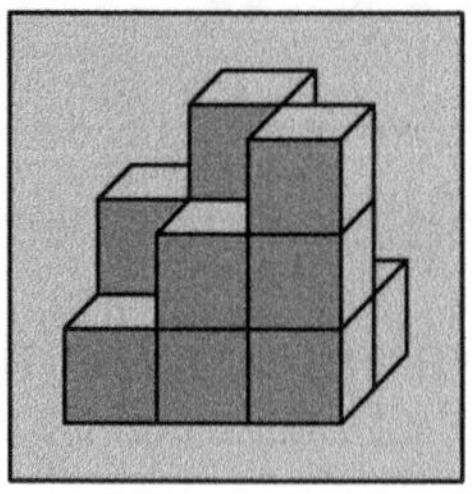

1

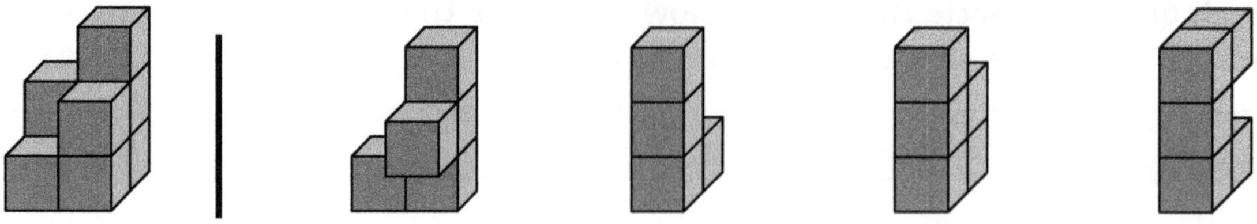

A B C D

2

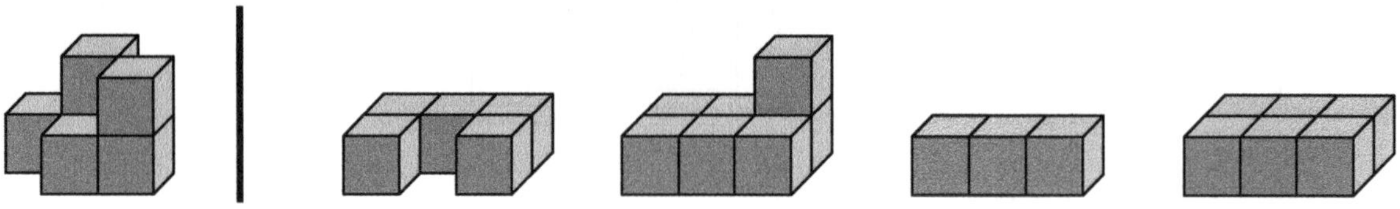

A B C D

3

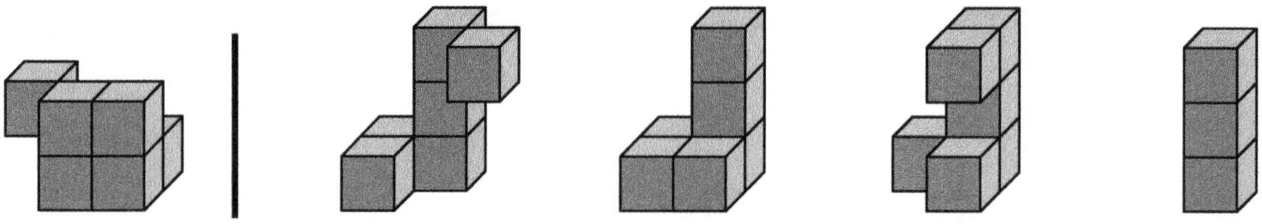

A B C D

4

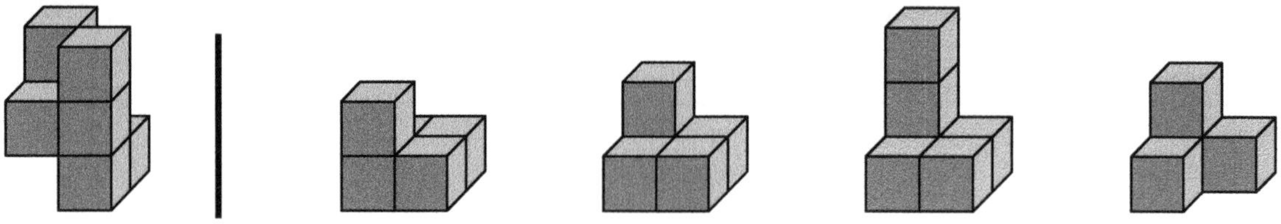

A B C D

5

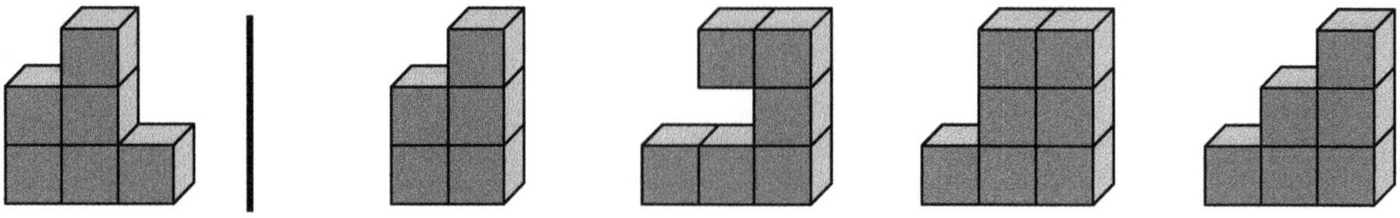

A B C D

Refer to the shape in the grey box for Questions 6–10 below.

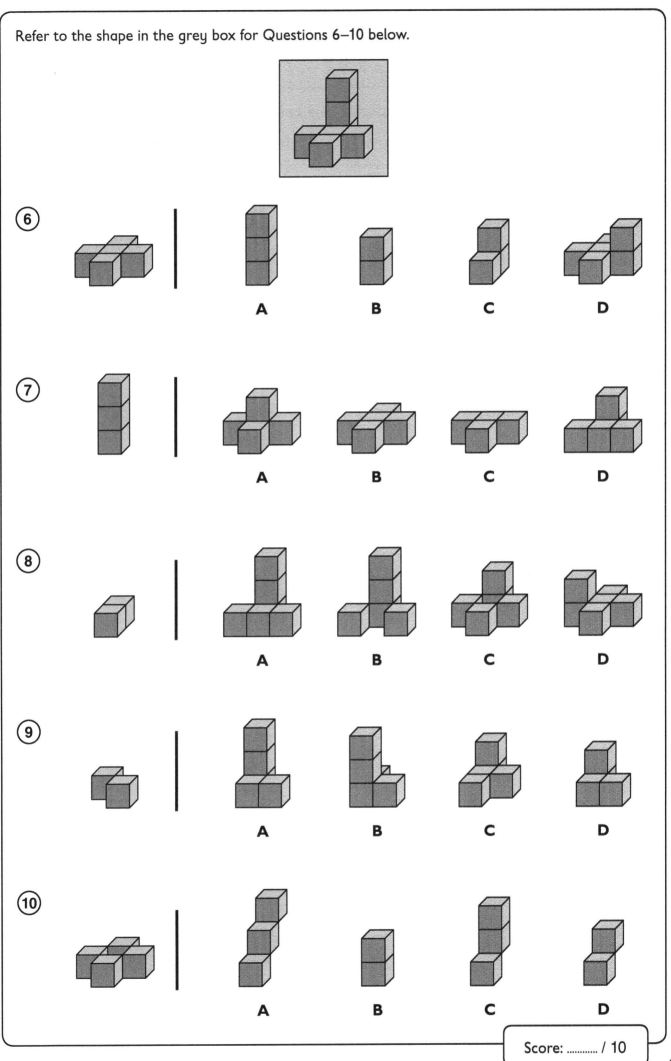

6

A   B   C   D

7

A   B   C   D

8

A   B   C   D

9

A   B   C   D

10

A   B   C   D

Score: .... / 10

Test 15

You have 6 minutes to complete this test.

You have 12 questions to complete within the given time.

In each question, one of the 3D figures below has been rotated to create the figure shown. Circle the letter of the figure that has been rotated.

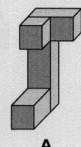

A

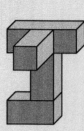

D

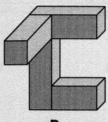

B

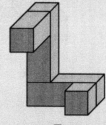

E

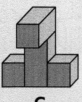

C

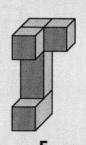

F

EXAMPLE

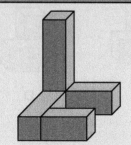

A	D
Ⓑ	E
C	F

 ①

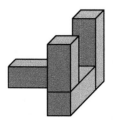

A	D
B	E
C	F

②

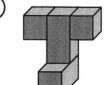

A	D
B	E
C	F

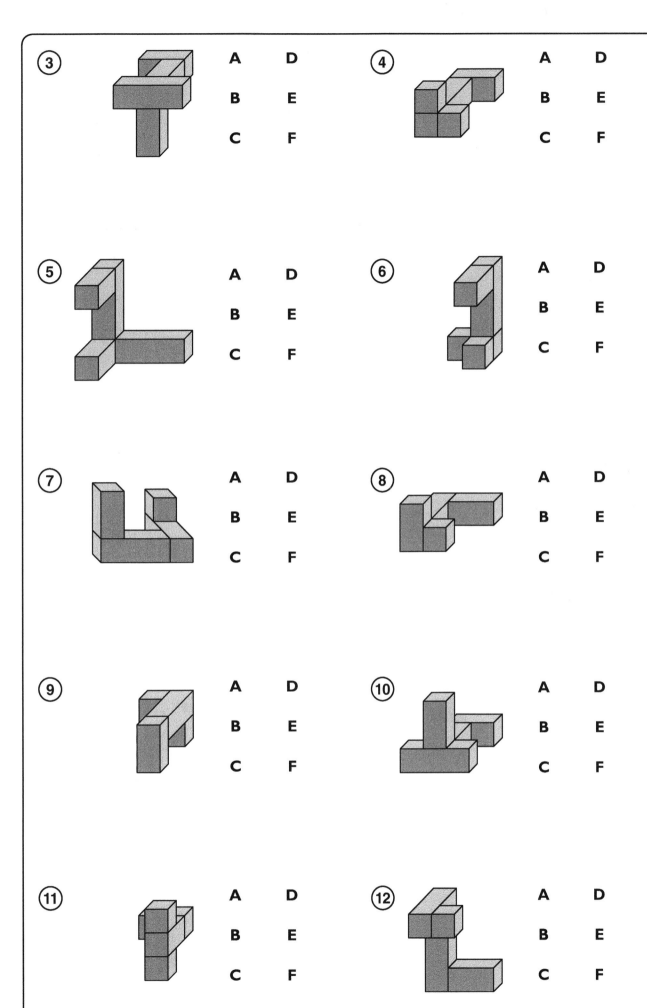

③   A   D   ④   A   D
     B   E   B   E
     C   F   C   F

⑤   A   D   ⑥   A   D
     B   E   B   E
     C   F   C   F

⑦   A   D   ⑧   A   D
     B   E   B   E
     C   F   C   F

⑨   A   D   ⑩   A   D
     B   E   B   E
     C   F   C   F

⑪   A   D   ⑫   A   D
     B   E   B   E
     C   F   C   F

Score: .... / 12

Test 16

You have 5 minutes to complete this test.

You have 10 questions to complete within the given time.

In each question, circle the letter below the figure that shows how the left-hand figure will look when folded along the dotted line.

The fold should be made towards the dotted line, not away from it.

EXAMPLE

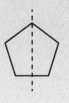

(A)   B   C   D

①

A   B   C   D

②

A   B   C   D

③

A   B   C   D

④

A   B   C   D

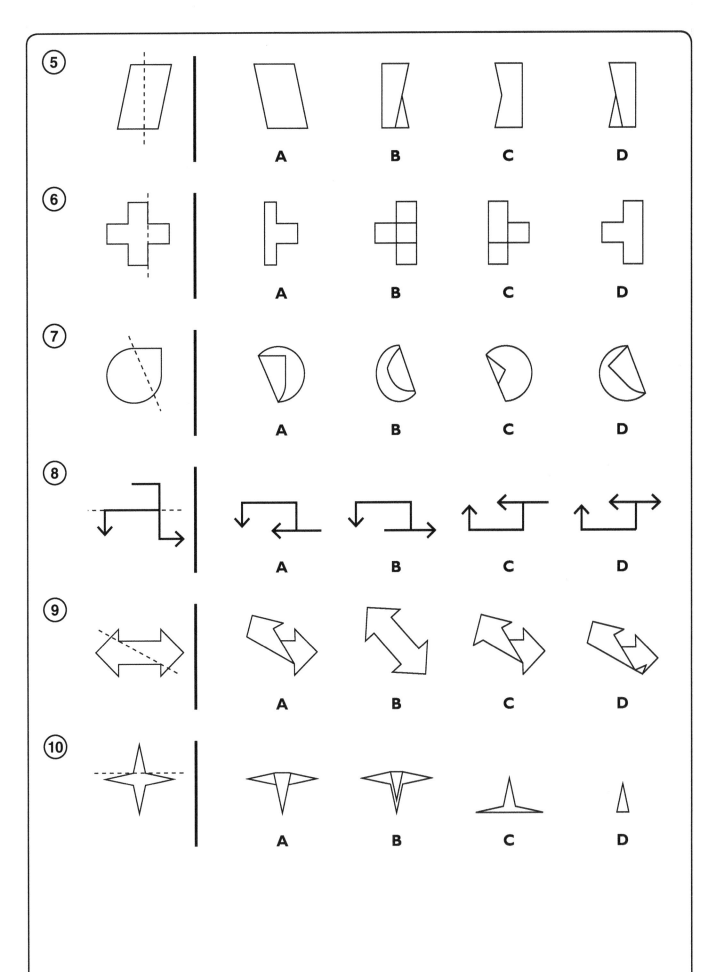

⑤   **A**   **B**   **C**   **D**

⑥   **A**   **B**   **C**   **D**

⑦   **A**   **B**   **C**   **D**

⑧   **A**   **B**   **C**   **D**

⑨   **A**   **B**   **C**   **D**

⑩   **A**   **B**   **C**   **D**

Score: .... / 10

45

Test 17

You have 5 minutes to complete this test.

You have 10 questions to complete within the given time.

In each question, the first row of figures shows how a square is folded and then holes are punched into it.

Circle the letter below the figure that correctly shows the unfolded square.

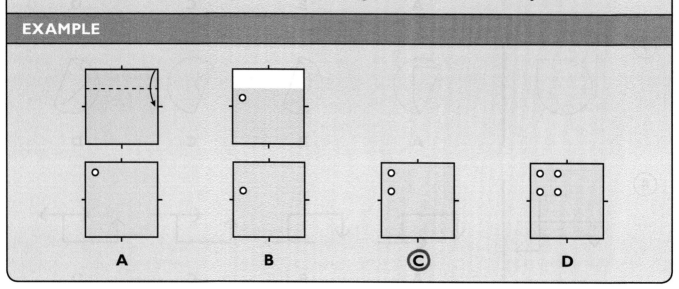

A   B   C   D

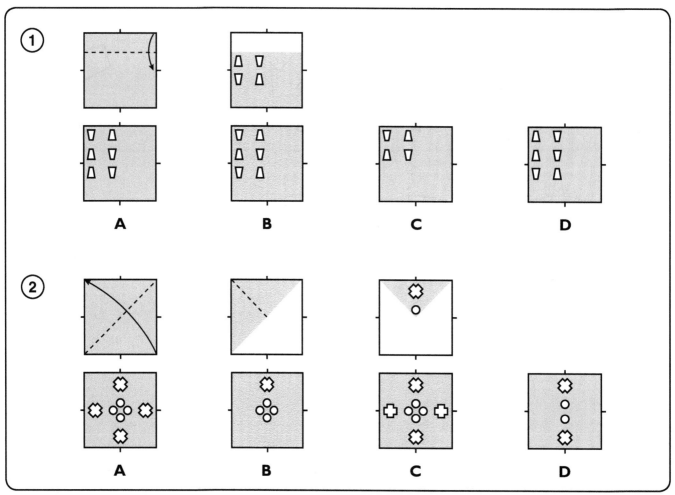

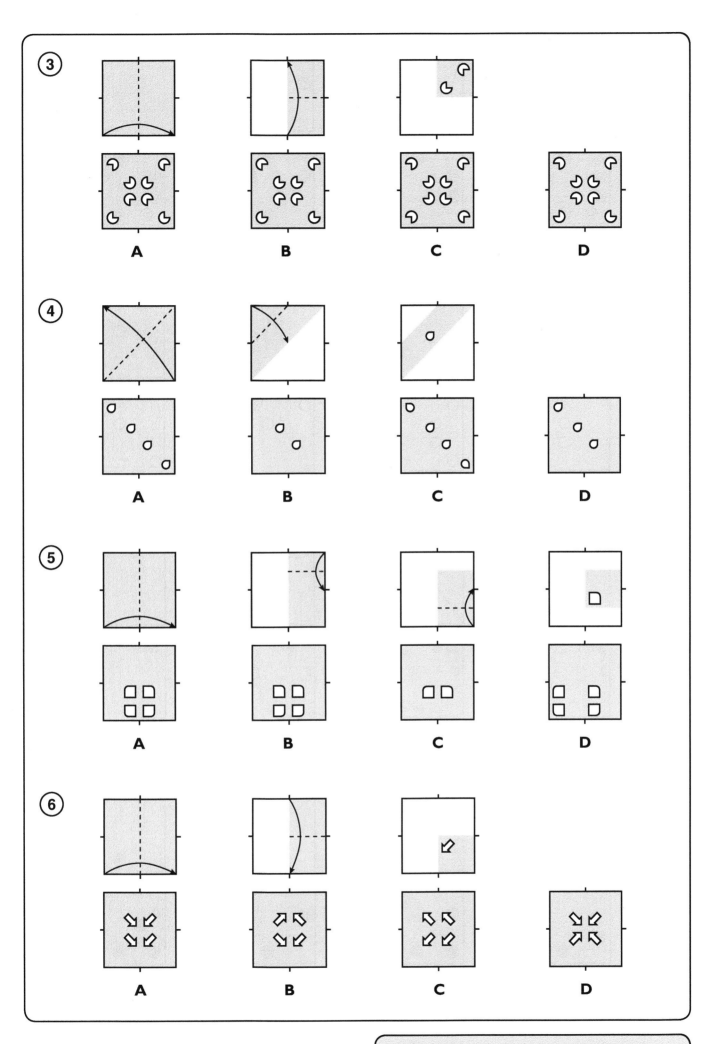

Questions continue on next page

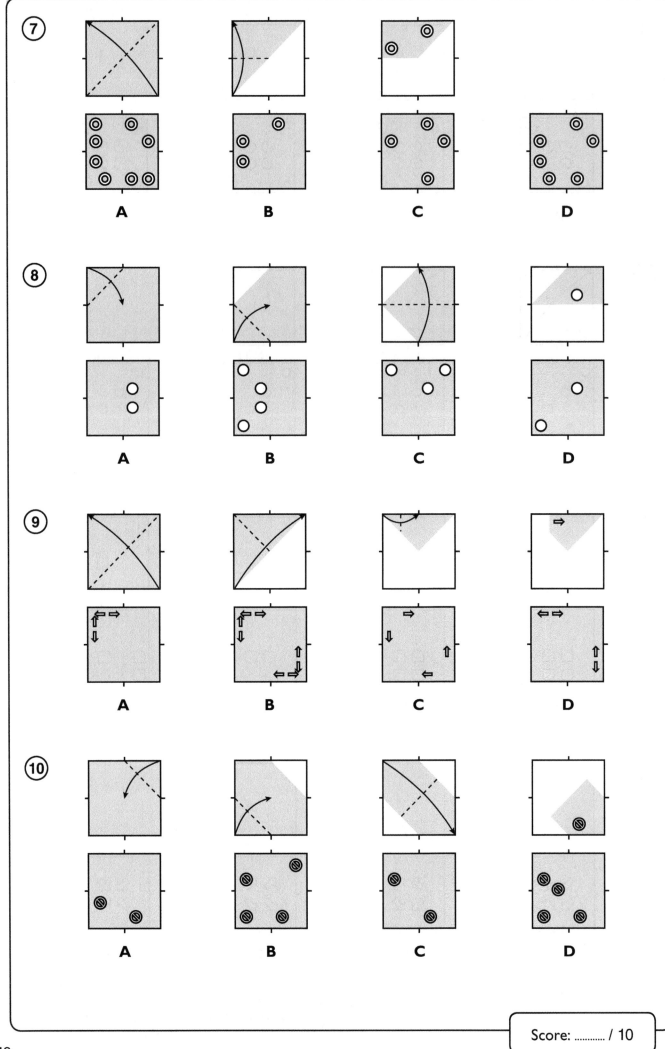

Score: .... / 10

Test 18

You have 5 minutes to complete this test.

You have 10 questions to complete within the given time.

In each question, circle the letter below the figure on the right that shows the 2D side view of the 3D figure on the left, when viewed from the **right**.

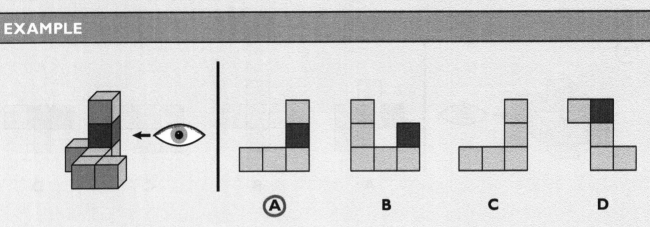

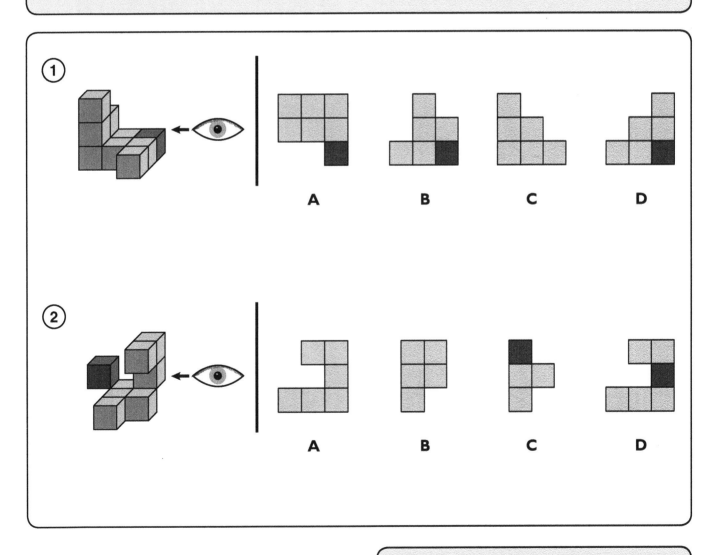

Questions continue on next page

49

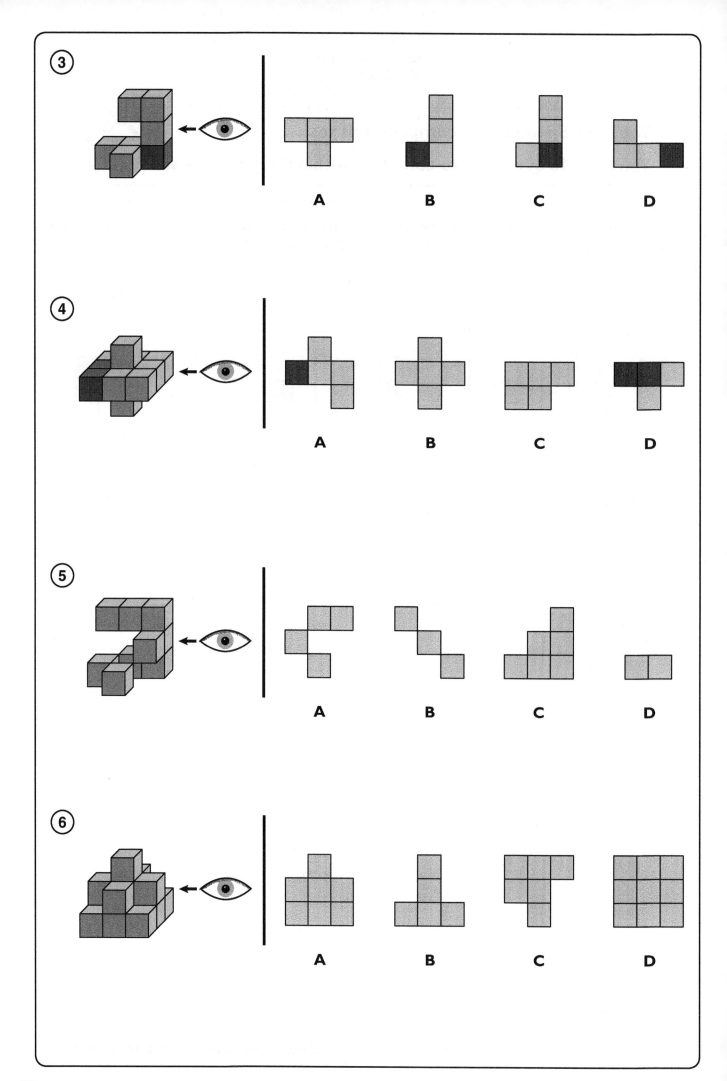

③

④

⑤

⑥

A B C D

50

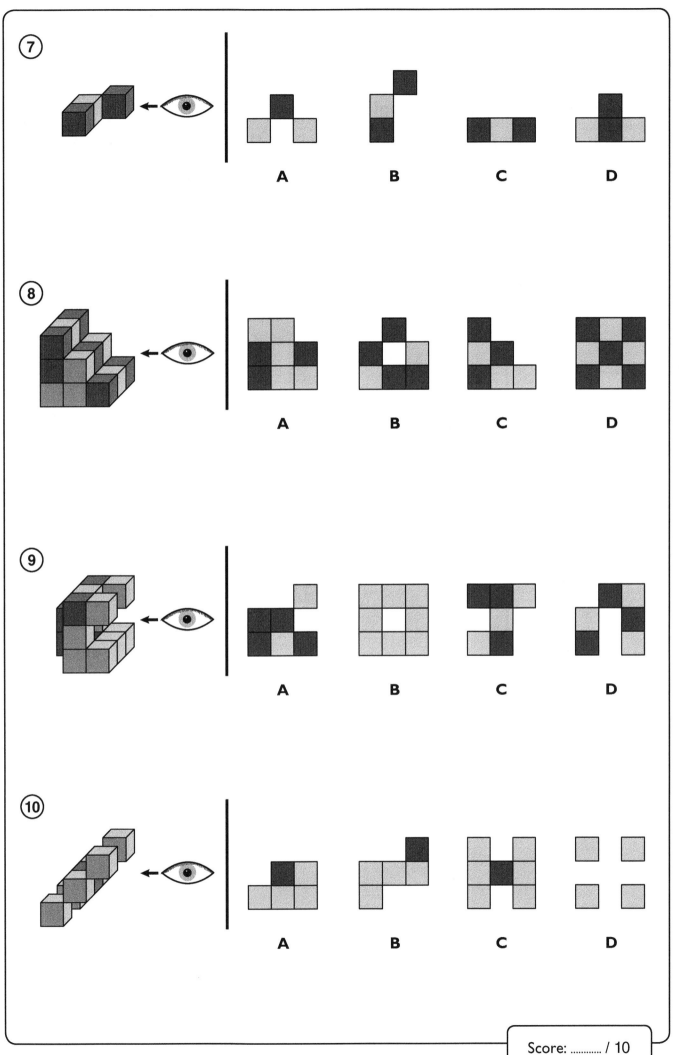

Test 19

You have 5 minutes to complete this test.

You have 10 questions to complete within the given time.

In each question, circle the letter below the figure that shows how the 3D figure on the left could look when viewed from <u>behind</u>.

EXAMPLE

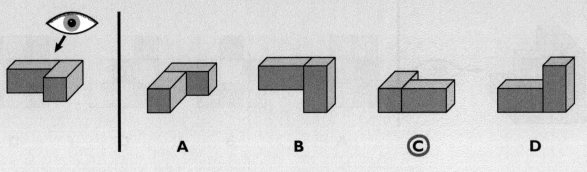

A   B   ©   D

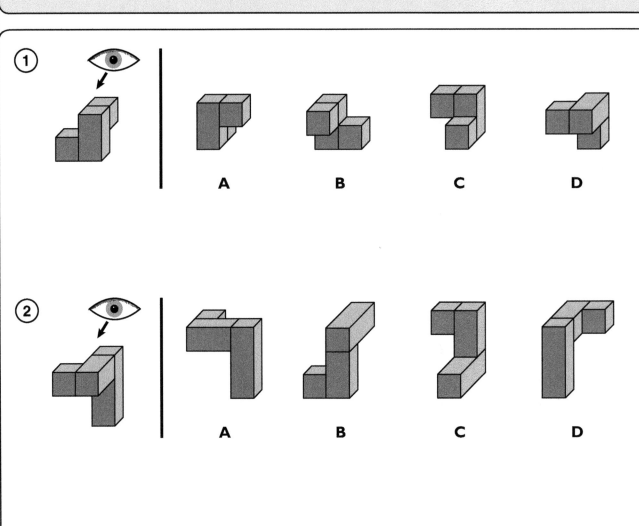

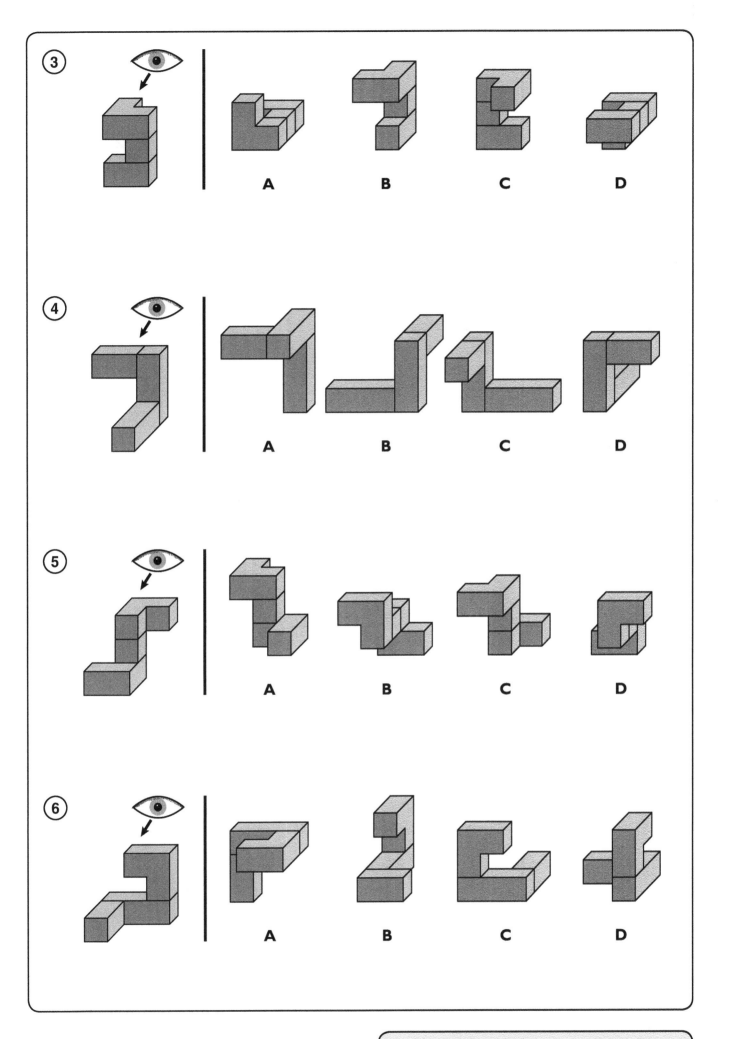

Questions continue on next page

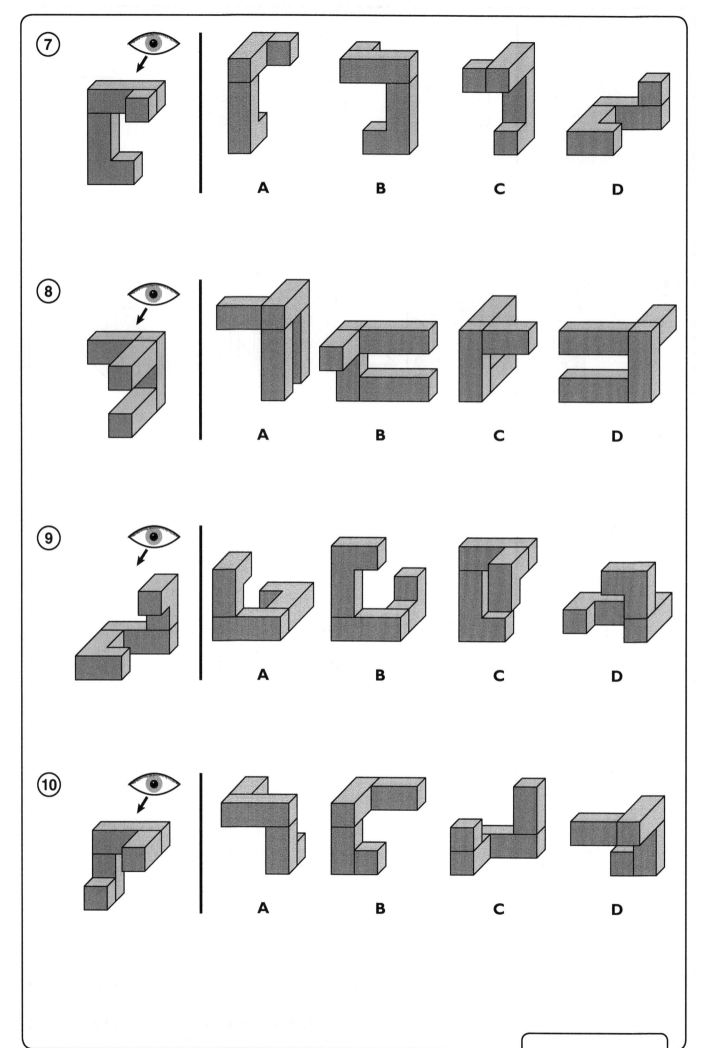

Test 20

You have 5 minutes to complete this test.

You have 10 questions to complete within the given time.

In each question, circle the letter below the cube that can be formed when folding the net on the left.

EXAMPLE

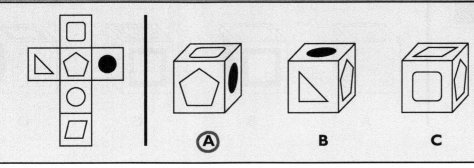

A (circled)   B   C   D

①
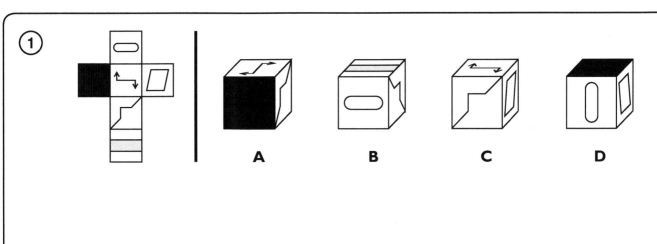

A   B   C   D

②
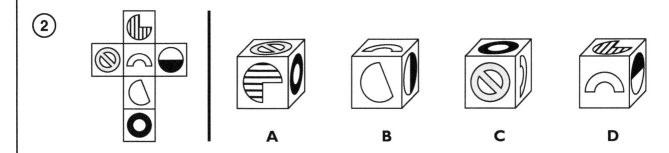

A   B   C   D

Questions continue on next page

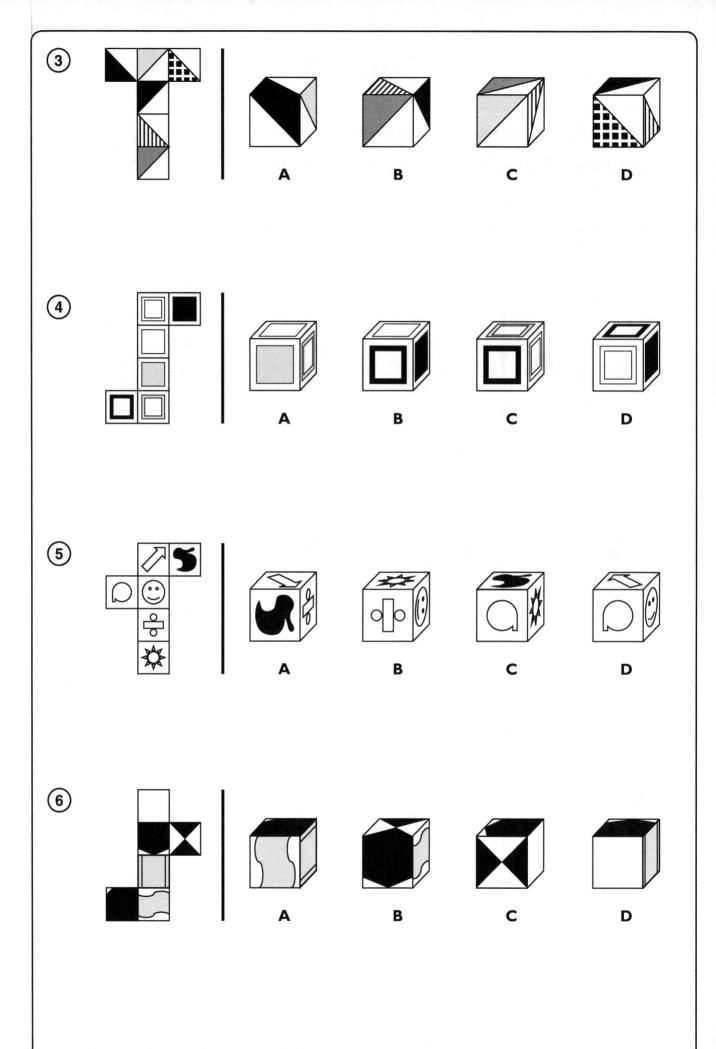

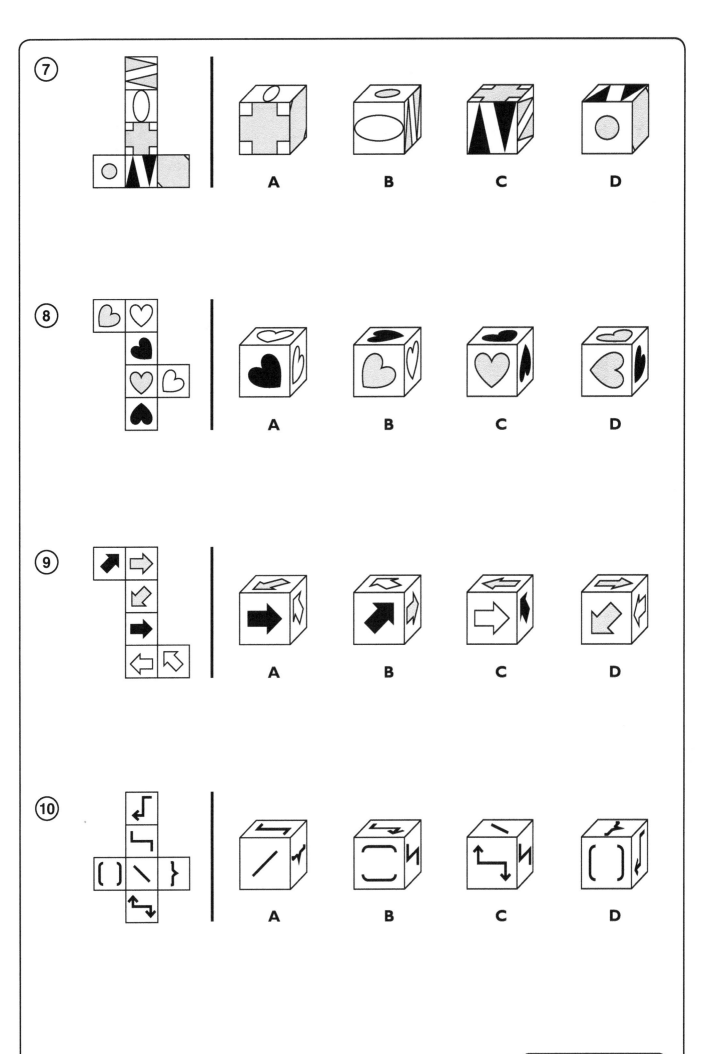

Test 21

You have 4 minutes to complete this test.

You have 8 questions to complete within the given time.

In each question, circle the letter below the net that can be folded to make the cube on the left.

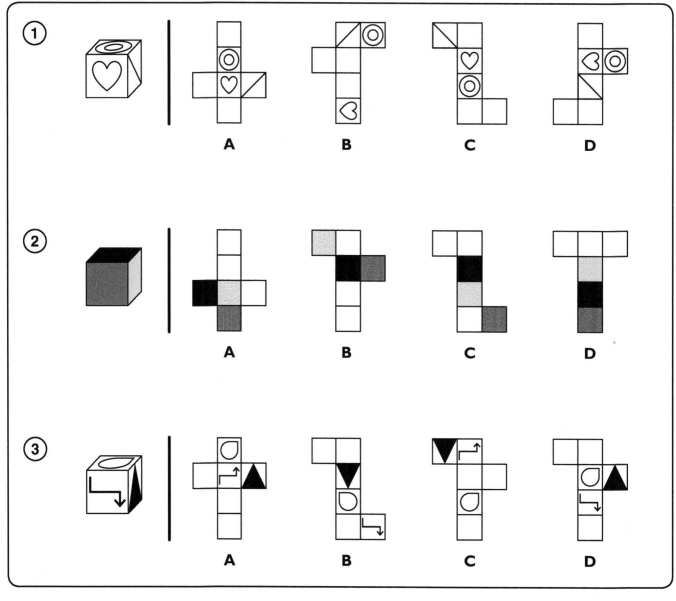

58

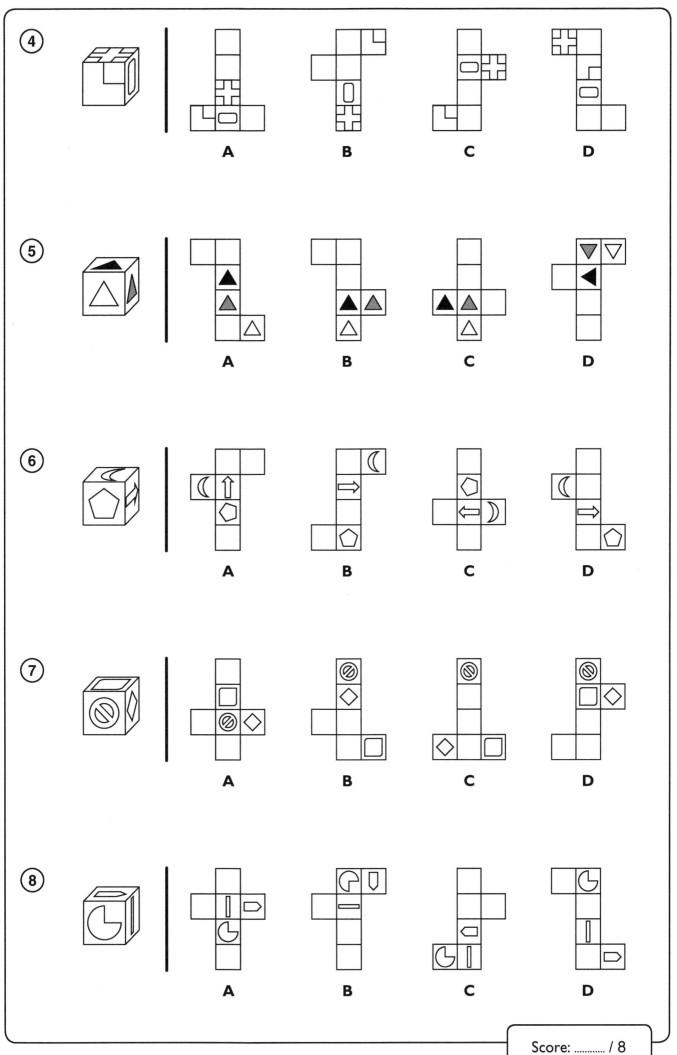

Test 22

You have 5 minutes to complete this test.

You have 10 questions to complete within the given time.

In each question, circle the letter below the 3D shape that can be formed from the net on the left.

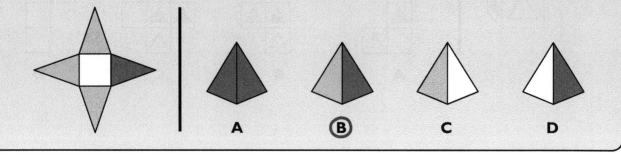

A   Ⓑ   C   D

---

① 

          A   B   C   D

② 

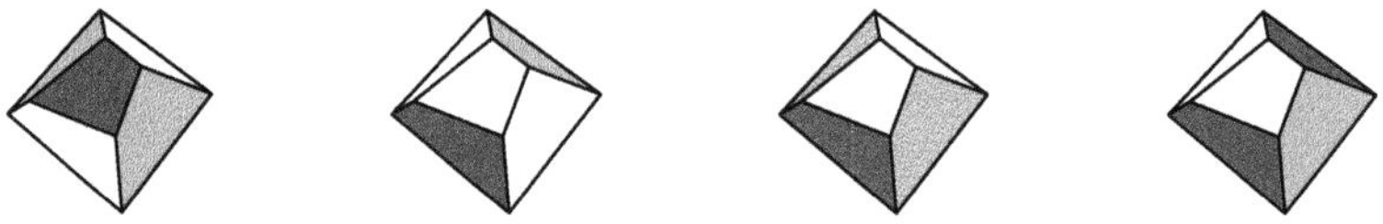

          A   B   C   D

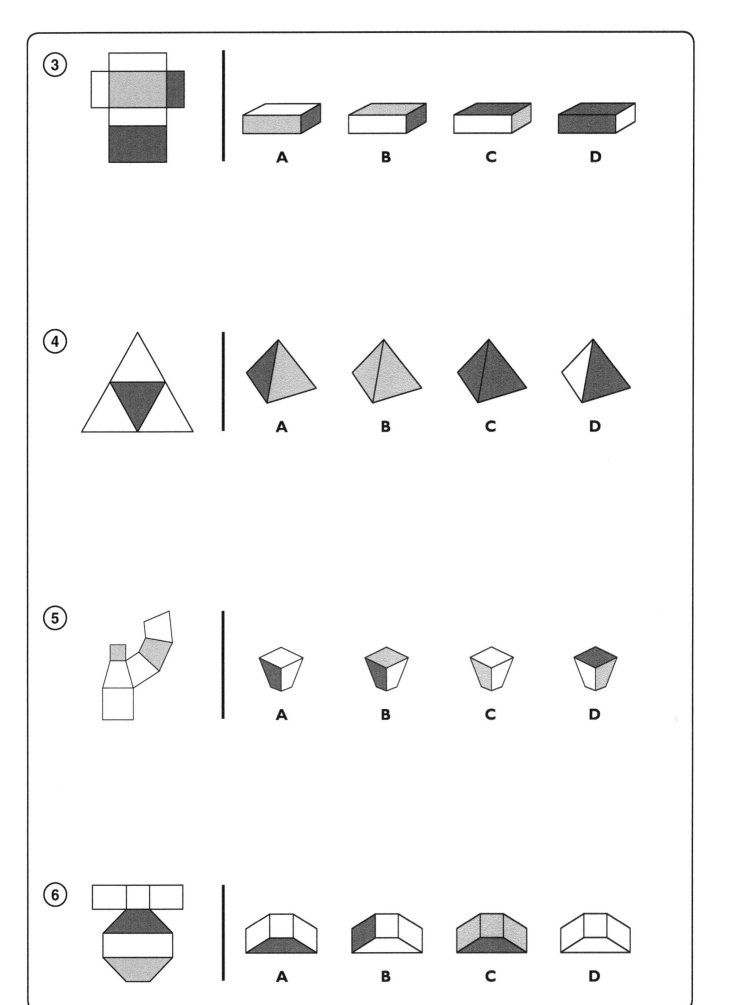

Questions continue on next page

⑦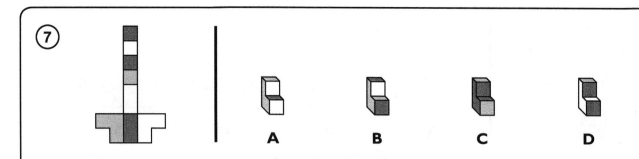

⑧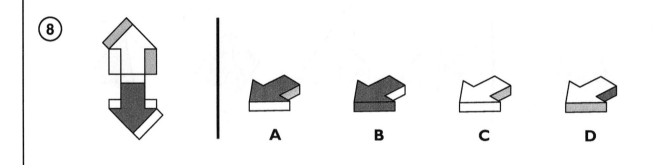

⑨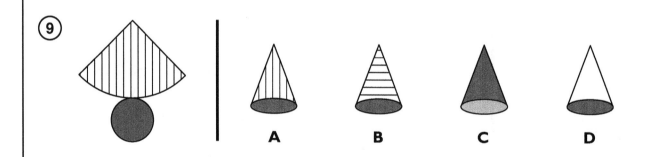

⑩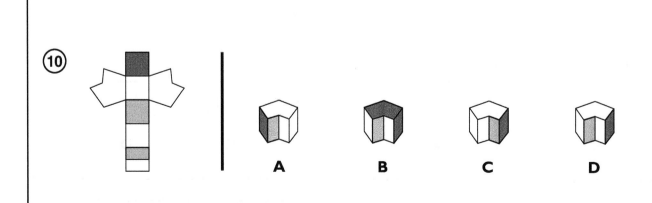

Score: .... / 10

62

Test 23

You have 5 minutes to complete this test.

You have 10 questions to complete within the given time.

In each question, the figures on the left show different views of the same cube.

Every face of this cube is different.

Circle the letter below the figure that should replace the blank face.

A   B   Ⓒ   D

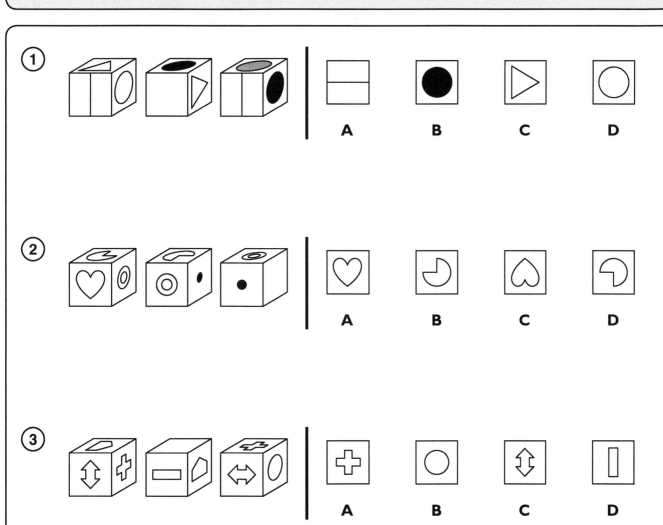

①   A   B   C   D

②   A   B   C   D

③   A   B   C   D

Questions continue on next page

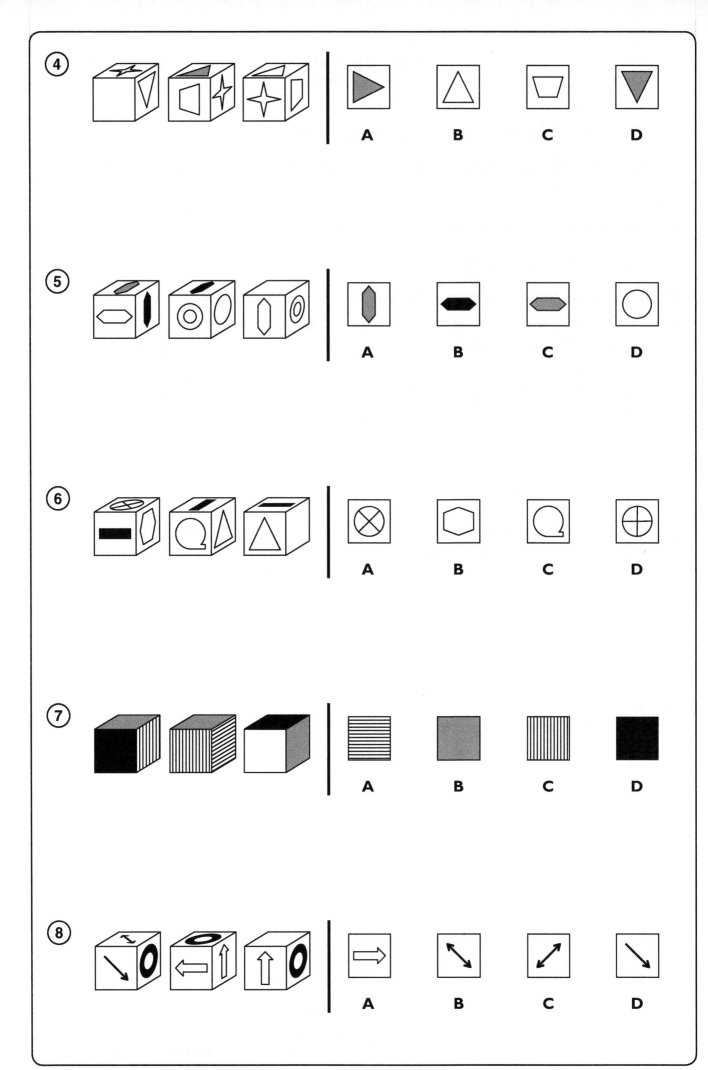

⑨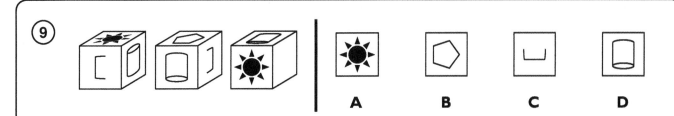

A   B   C   D

⑩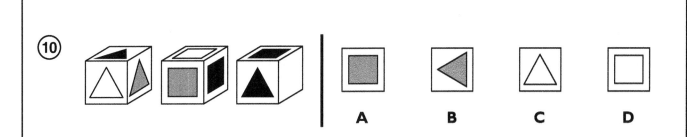

A   B   C   D

Test 24

In each question, the shape on the left is hidden in one of the figures on the right.

This shape stays exactly the same size and does not get rotated or flipped over.

Circle the letter below the figure that contains the hidden shape.

EXAMPLE

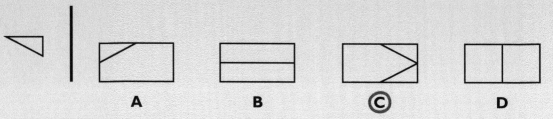

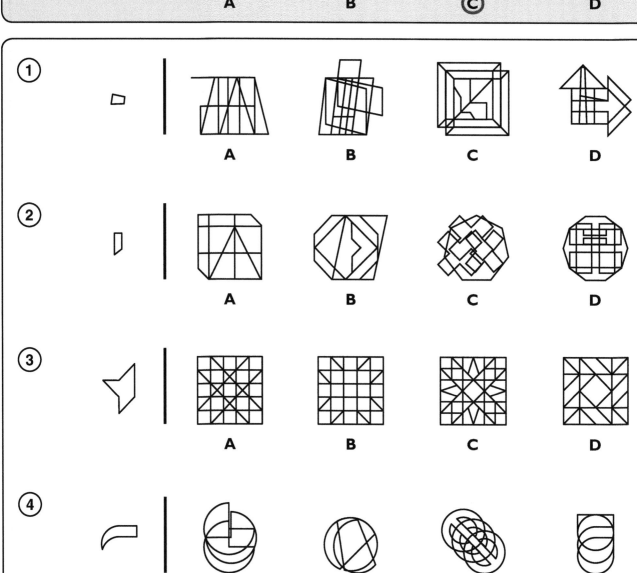

66

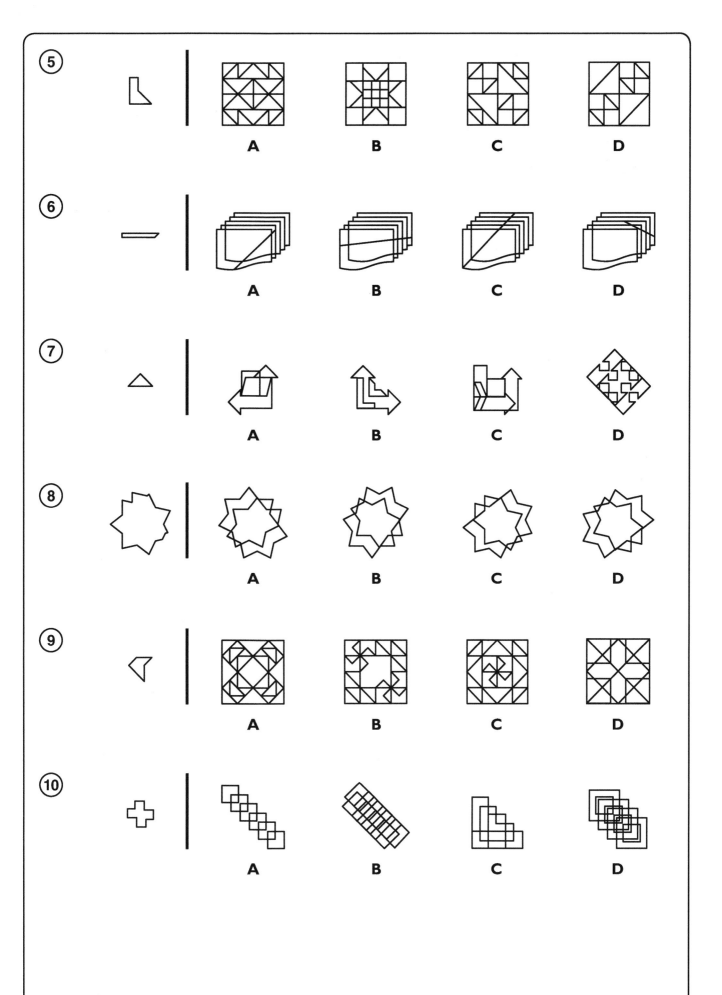

Test 25

You have 5 minutes to complete this test.

You have 10 questions to complete within the given time.

In each question, circle the letter below the figure on the right that shows the **2D rear view** of the 3D figure on the left.

EXAMPLE

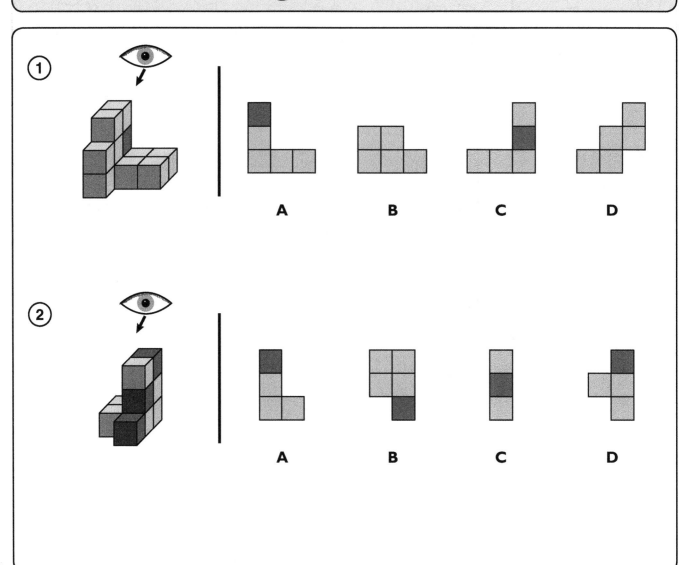

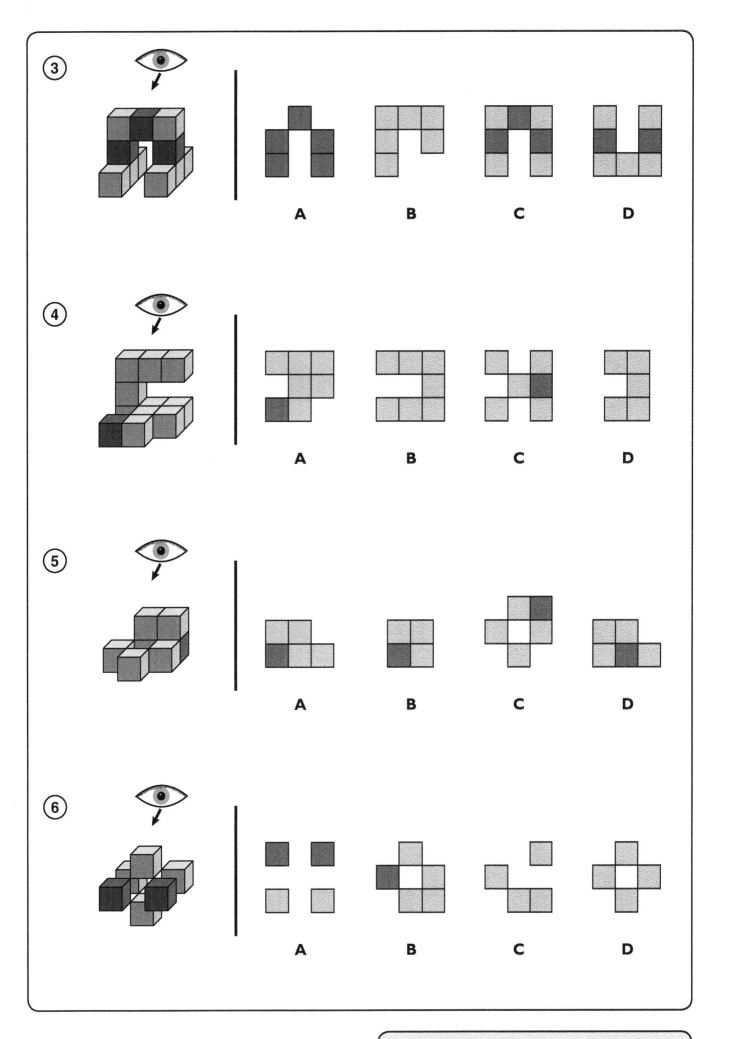

Questions continue on next page

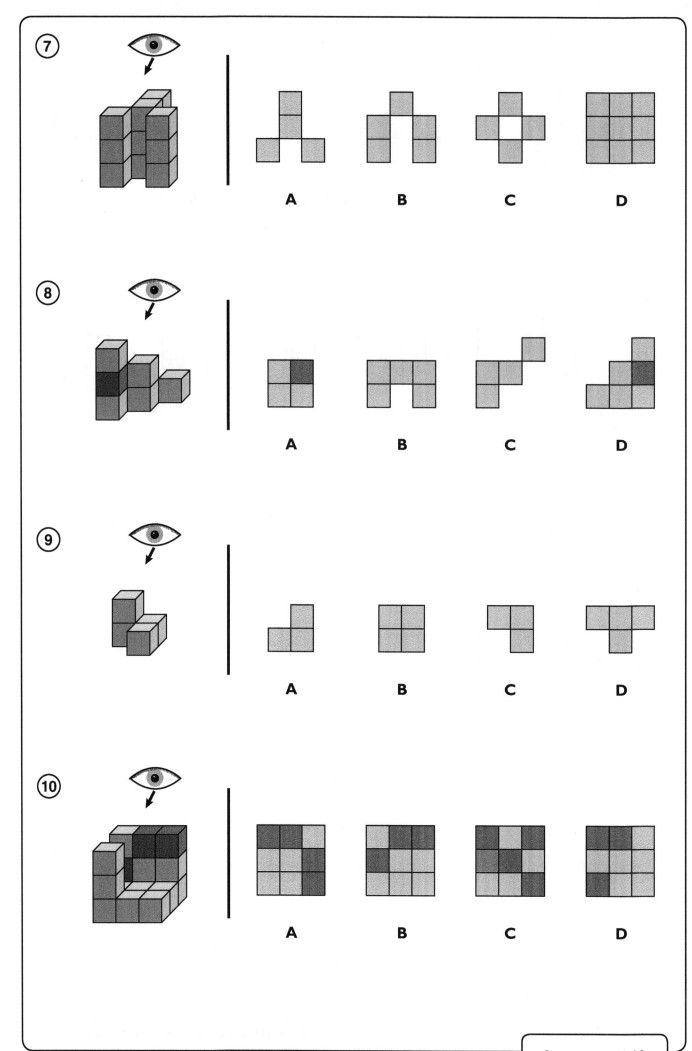

Score: .... / 10

Answers

Test 1

Q1 D

Q2 B

Q3 D

Q4 B

Q5 A

Q6 C

Q7 A

Q8 D

Q9 C

Q10 A

Q11 A

Q12 B

Test 2

Q1 B

Q2 A

Q3 C

Q4 A

Q5 A

Q6 C

Q7 B

Q8 D

Q9 B

Q10 D

Test 3

Q1 E
A 90° horizontal rotation clockwise. A 180° vertical rotation.

Q2 B
A 90° horizontal rotation anticlockwise. A 180° vertical rotation.

Q3 C
A 90° horizontal rotation clockwise. A 90° vertical rotation forwards.

Q4 A
A 180° horizontal rotation.

Q5 E
A 90° horizontal rotation anticlockwise. A 180° vertical rotation.

Q6 D
A 90° horizontal rotation anticlockwise. A 90° vertical rotation backwards.

Q7 F
A 90° horizontal rotation anticlockwise. A 90° vertical rotation forwards.

Q8 D
A 90° horizontal rotation clockwise.

Q9 B
A 90° horizontal rotation clockwise. A 90° vertical rotation backwards.

Q10 C
A 180° horizontal rotation.

Q11 A
A 90° horizontal rotation clockwise. A 90° vertical rotation forwards.

Q12 F
A 90° horizontal rotation clockwise. A 180° vertical rotation.

Test 4

Q1 C
The left-hand side folds over the right-hand side.

Q2 B
The left-hand side folds directly on top of the right-hand side.

Q3 C
The right-hand side folds on top of the left-hand side.

Q4 A
The bottom section folds on top of the top section.

Q5 D
The bottom section folds over the top section.

Q6 B
The bottom section folds over the top section.

Q7 C
The top right section folds over the bottom left section.

Test 4 answers continue on next page

Q8 B

The left-hand side folds over the right-hand side.

Q9 A

The right-hand side folds on top of the left-hand side.

Q10 B

The right-hand side folds on top of the left-hand side.

Test 5

Q1 C

Q2 A

Q3 C

Q4 D

Q5 A

Q6 D

Q7 A

Q8 D

Q9 D

Q10 C

Test 6

Q1 B

The shape has 6 blocks visible from above, which rules out A and C. There are no dark blocks visible from above, which rules out D.

Q2 C

There are 6 blocks visible from above, which rules out D. There is 1 dark block visible from above, which rules out A. When viewed from above, the dark block is at the top of a column of 4 blocks on the left. This rules out B.

Q3 A

When viewed from above, there is a block in the middle of the shape, which rules out B and C. The block in the middle is light, which rules out D.

Q4 C

When viewed from above, the block at the top of the middle column is dark, which rules out B and D. There is a light block to the right of this dark block, which rules out A.

Q5 A

When viewed from above, the block in the top right is dark, which rules out B and D. There is a light block below the dark block, which rules out C.

Q6 D

The shape has 8 blocks visible from above, which rules out A and C. The shape has 1 dark block visible from above, which rules out B.

Q7 D

The shape has 7 blocks visible from above, which rules out A, B and C.

Q8 A

The shape has 8 blocks visible from above, which rules out B and C. The shape has no dark blocks visible from above, which rules out D.

Q9 D

When viewed from above, the shape has a 2-block hole in the middle, which rules out B and C. The shape has no dark block in the right-hand column when viewed from above, which rules out A.

Q10 C

The shape has 7 blocks visible from above, which rules out B and D. The shape has 1 dark block visible from above, which rules out A.

Test 7

Q1 A

When viewed from the top, the closest face to the viewer is horizontal and 2 blocks wide. This rules out B, C and D.

Q2 C

When viewed from the top, 3 cubed-shape faces are closest to the viewer. This rules out A, B and D.

Q3 D

When viewed from the top, there is a column 2 blocks high closest to the viewer. This rules out A, B and C.

Q4 C

When viewed from the top, there is a column 3 blocks high on the left with 1 block in front of it. This rules out A, B and D.

Q5 C

When viewed from the top, there is a column 2 blocks high on the left. This rules out A, B and D.

Q6 B

When viewed from the top, there is a row 3 blocks wide on the face closest to the viewer. This rules out A, C and D.

Q7 B

When viewed from the top, the face closest to the viewer consists of a row 3 blocks wide. This rules out A, C and D.

Q8 D

When viewed from the top, the face closest to the viewer includes a column 5 blocks high. This rules out A, B and C.

Q9 C

When viewed from the top, there is a column 2 blocks high on the right closest to the viewer. This rules out A, B and D.

Q10 B

When viewed from the top, there is a column 3 blocks high on the left. This rules out A, C and D.

Test 8

Q1 C

Q2 A

Q3 A

Q4 B

Q5 C

Q6 B

Q7 B

Q8 D

Q9 C

Q10 D

Test 9

Q1 C

Q2 B

Q3 C

Q4 D

Q5 B

Q6 C

Q7 A

Q8 C

Test 10

Q1 A

The small triangle at the top of the shape is grey, which rules out B and C. The shape only has 1 dark trapezium-shaped face, which rules out D.

Q2 C

The shape has 2 small white squares, which rules out A and B. The shape has 2 grey non-square faces, which rules out D which has 3 such faces.

Q3 B

For the light grey trapezium-shaped face to be on the top in this orientation, the white rectangular face must be on the left, which rules out A, C and D.

Q4 D

The star-shaped faces are white, which rules out B. Alternate rectangular faces are grey and white, which rules out A and C.

Q5 B

The triangular faces are white and light grey, which rules out A. The rectangular faces are white and dark grey, which rules out C and D.

Q6 A

There are not 2 triangular faces the same colour next to each other, which rules out B, C and D.

Q7 D

The curved part of the shape is white, which rules out A, B and C.

Q8 B

The 2 light grey rectangular faces are not separated by only 1 white rectangular face, which rules out A. If the light grey hexagon-shaped face is on the top, there is a light grey rectangular face directly to the right of the dark grey rectangular face, which rules out C. There is only 1 dark grey rectangular face, which rules out D.

Q9 D

The pentagon-shaped faces are white and dark grey, which rules out B. If the white pentagon-shaped face is on the left, the face on the top must be dark grey, which rules out A. If the dark grey pentagon-shaped face is on the left, the face on the top must be white, which rules out C.

Q10 A

The larger faces of the shape are all white, which rules out B, C and D.

Test 11

Q1 B

Q2 A

Q3 B

Q4 A

Q5 C

Test 11 answers continue on next page

Q6   C

Q7   B

Q8   B

Q9   A

Q10 A

Test 12

Q1   B

Q2   C

Q3   C

Q4   B

Q5   A

Q6   D

Q7   D

Q8   C

Q9   B

Q10 C

Test 13

Q1   A

Q2   B

Q3   B

Q4   D

Q5   C

Q6   B

Q7   A

Q8   B

Q9   C

Q10 B

Q11 A

Q12 D

Test 14

Q1   B

Q2   D

Q3   A

Q4   B

Q5   D

Q6   B

Q7   C

Q8   B

Q9   A

Q10 C

Test 15

Q1   B
A 90° horizontal rotation clockwise. A 90° vertical rotation backwards.

Q2   C
A 180° horizontal rotation. A 180° vertical rotation.

Q3   D
A 90° vertical rotation forwards.

Q4   F
A 90° horizontal rotation anticlockwise. A 90° vertical rotation forwards.

Q5   B
A 90° horizontal rotation anticlockwise. A 180° vertical rotation.

Q6   A
A 180° horizontal rotation. A 180° vertical rotation.

Q7   E
A 90° vertical rotation backwards. A 90° horizontal rotation anticlockwise.

Q8   A
A 90° horizontal rotation anticlockwise. A 90° vertical rotation forwards.

Q9   F
A 180° horizontal rotation. A 90° vertical rotation backwards.

Q10 D
A 180° horizontal rotation. A 90° vertical rotation forwards.

Q11 C
A 90° horizontal rotation clockwise. A 90° vertical rotation backwards.

Q12 E
A 90° horizontal rotation anticlockwise. A 180° vertical rotation.

Test 16

Q1 A
The top section folds over the dotted line.

Q2 A
The bottom section folds up over the top section.

Q3 B
The bottom section folds up over the top section.

Q4 A
The top left section folds over the bottom right section.

Q5 D
The right section folds over the left section.

Q6 B
The right section folds over the left section.

Q7 D
The right section folds over the left section.

Q8 B
The top section folds over the bottom section.

Q9 D
The bottom left section folds over the top right section.

Q10 B
The top section folds over the bottom section.

Test 17

Q1 B

Q2 A

Q3 D

Q4 A

Q5 A

Q6 B

Q7 D

Q8 A

Q9 B

Q10 C

Test 18

Q1 B
The shape has 6 blocks visible from the right, which rules out A. When viewed from the right, the shape has 2 blocks in the column on the right, which rules out C and D.

Q2 A
The shape has 6 blocks visible from the right, which rules out B and C. The shape has no dark blocks visible from the right, which rules out D.

Q3 C
The shape has 1 dark block visible from the right, which rules out A. When viewed from the right, the dark block is the bottom block in a column of 3 on the right. This rules out B and D.

Q4 B
The shape has 5 blocks visible from the right, which rules out D. The shape has no dark blocks visible from the right, which rules out A. When viewed from the right, the shape has a column 3 blocks high in the middle, which rules out C.

Q5 C
The shape has 6 blocks visible from the right, which rules out A, B and D.

Q6 A
The shape has 7 blocks visible from the right, which rules out B, C and D.

Q7 C
The shape has 3 blocks visible from the right, which rules out D. These blocks are all in the same row, which rules out A and B.

Q8 D
The shape has 9 blocks visible from the right, which rules out A, B and C.

Q9 B
When viewed from the right, the shape has a row of 3 light blocks at the bottom, which rules out A, C and D.

Q10 C
When viewed from the right, the shape has a column 3 blocks high on the left, which rules out A, B and D.

Test 19

Q1 B
When viewed from the back, the right-hand column has 1 block, which is on the bottom row. This rules out A, C and D.

Q2 D
When viewed from the back, the left-hand column is 3 blocks high. This rules out A, B and C.

Q3 C
When viewed from the back, the left-hand column is 3 blocks high. This rules out A, B and D.

Test 19 answers continue on next page

Q4 D

When viewed from the back, the face closest to the viewer on the left-hand side is 3 blocks high. This rules out A, B and C.

Q5 C

When viewed from the back, the face closest to the viewer is rectangular, 2 blocks wide and 1 block high. This rules out A, B and D.

Q6 C

When viewed from the back, the face closest to the viewer on the left-hand side is 3 blocks high. This rules out A, B and D.

Q7 B

When viewed from the back, the face closest to the viewer on the right-hand side is 4 blocks high. This rules out A, C and D.

Q8 C

When viewed from the back, the face closest to the viewer on the left-hand side is 3 blocks high. This rules out A, B and D.

Q9 A

When viewed from the back, the left-hand face is 3 blocks high. This rules out B, C and D.

Q10 A

When viewed from the back, the right-hand face closest to the viewer is 3 blocks high. This rules out B, C and D.

Test 20

Q1	A
Q2	A
Q3	A
Q4	C
Q5	D
Q6	C
Q7	B
Q8	D
Q9	C
Q10	B

Test 21

Q1	B
Q2	A
Q3	B

Q4	B
Q5	D
Q6	A
Q7	B
Q8	B

Test 22

Q1 A

The light grey trapezium-shaped face should have a white face to its right and a dark grey face to its left, which rules out B and D. There is no white trapezium-shaped face with a light grey face to its left and a dark grey face to its right, which rules out C.

Q2 C

The face at the top of the shape is white, which rules out A. 2 of the faces around the top face are light grey, which rules out B and D.

Q3 B

The large faces are light grey and dark grey, which rules out A. The other faces are white or dark grey, which rules out C. The longer faces on the side of the shape are both white, which rules out D.

Q4 D

The shape has no light grey faces, which rules out A and B. The shape has only 1 dark grey face, which rules out C.

Q5 C

The shape has no dark grey faces, which rules out A, B and D.

Q6 A

All the rectangular faces of the shape are white, which rules out B and C. The 2 trapezium-shaped faces are not white, which rules out D.

Q7 D

The L-shaped face is either white or light grey which rules out C. If the white L-shaped face is to the left, the two squares facing up must be light grey and white, which rules out A and B.

Q8 A

The rectangular faces of the shape are white or light grey, which rules out B and D. If the arrow-shaped face on top of the shape is white, the rectangular face closest to the viewer must be light grey, which rules out C.

Q9 A
The curved face of the shape has vertical striped lines, which rules out B, C and D.

Q10 D
The top face of the shape is white, which rules out B. The dark grey face has a white face on either side of it, which rules out A and C.

Test 23

Q1 A

Q2 B

Q3 A

Q4 C

Q5 B

Q6 B

Q7 A

Q8 D

Q9 C

Q10 B

Test 24

Q1 B

Q2 D

Q3 D

Q4 D

Q5 B

Q6 C

Q7 A

Q8 C

Q9 A

Q10 A

Test 25

Q1 C
When viewed from the back, the shape has a column 1 block high in the middle, which rules out B and D. There is no dark block in the left column, which rules out A.

Q2 A
The shape has 4 blocks visible from the back, which rules out B and C. When viewed from the back, the shape has a column 3 blocks high on the left, which rules out D.

Q3 C
The shape has 7 blocks visible from the back, which rules out A and B. When viewed from the back, the top row of the shape consists of 3 blocks, which rules out D.

Q4 B
The shape has 7 blocks visible from the back, which rules out C and D. The shape has no dark blocks visible from the back, which rules out A.

Q5 A
The shape has 5 blocks visible from the back, which rules out B. When viewed from the back, the dark block is in the bottom left corner, which rules out C and D.

Q6 D
The shape has 4 blocks visible from the back, which rules outs B. None of these blocks is dark, which rules out A. When viewed from the back, there is 1 block in the bottom row which rules out C.

Q7 D
The shape has 9 blocks visible from the back, which rules out A, B and C.

Q8 D
The shape has 6 blocks visible from the back, which rules out A, B and C.

Q9 A
The shape has 3 blocks visible from the back, which rules out B and D. When viewed from the back, the shape has a bottom row with 2 blocks, which rules out C.

Q10 A
When viewed from the back, there are 2 dark blocks in the middle and left of the top row. This rules out B and C. When viewed from the back, there is a dark block on the right of the middle row, which rules out D.

Notes

Notes

Notes